It Is Enough!

It Is Enough!
Singing Oratorio Aria for Baritone, Handel and Mendelssohn
by Yuman Lee, DMA

Edited by Rachel Newman

ISBN-13: 978-1732448667
ISBN-10: 1732448663

Published by:
Lazarus Tribe Media, LLC
Rome, Georgia

Printed in the United States of America

Publisher's Site: www.lazarustribemedia.com
Author's Page: www.lazarustribemedia.com/yumanlee

It Is Enough!
Singing Oratorio Aria for Baritone
- Handel and Mendelssohn -

by Yuman Lee, DMA

Lazarus Tribe Media
Rome, Georgia

To my beautiful wife, Myung Hee Ha,
and to my three lovely children,
Joseph,
Elizabeth,
and Anna,
as well as to my parents and parents-in-law.

Table of Contents

Examples

Tables

1
Introduction

In the course of their daily lives, people experience and reveal a variety of emotions, ranging from sadness, anger, and rage, to desire and love, all of which can be expressed through language and behavior. Deep feelings, however, can also be conveyed through the singing voice. Singing has developed over the centuries as a creative tool of expression and communication, one that relates to what a person (or character) feels and believes, either in real life or in a singer's performance on stage. Whereas almost anyone can make a musical sound of sorts without vocal training, the perfection of singing requires continual technical development, so that performers can convey these powerful emotions in a way that moves an audience. This expression of "feeling" via musical vocal sound, what we normally refer to as singing, is a unique human feature and God's gift to His children, a gift that allows the human spirit to take flight toward the divine and to soar.

To demonstrate this relationship between the singer, his vocal craft, and the audience, this feeling-sound-feeling correspondence, a discussion is presented based on a selection of eleven bass-baritone oratorio arias containing themes of rage, lament, and prayer (reverence), composed by George Frideric Handel and Felix Mendelssohn.

At present, no other such study of baritone or bass-baritone oratorio arias by Handel and Mendelssohn exists, especially in connection with the composer's lives and the social, intellectual, and musical influences of their day, which could shed light on how these arias should be sung. Consequently, a useful *pedagogical* perspective is an additional result of the research presented in this text. In other words, this book provides not only a repertoire resource of oratorio arias for baritone and bass-baritone singers, but also offers some helpful suggestions to teachers of singing.

There are numerous types of arias in oratorios, and presented here are selected arias for the low male voice that express the emotions of rage, lament, and prayer (reverence). Composers in the past normally designated "low male voice" as "bass," yet there were no specifications as to whether arias were written for baritone, bass-baritone, or bass. However, the arias included in this text from the oratorios of Handel and Mendelssohn are more appropriate for a baritone and bass-baritone rather than for a bass.

The reader will find the original text of each oratorio aria, whether or not the text is based on exact words from Scripture or paraphrased. Discussion of the original key(s) of each aria, as well as the *tessitura*, tempo, character's role, librettist, musical form, style, meter, orchestration, tonal structure, and some vocal techniques is included. The research presented in this text mainly relies on Friedrich Chrysander's editions of Handel's works as well as on Mendelssohn's versions. Much evidence shows that Mendelssohn edited, published, and conducted Handel's oratorios during his active career in England and Germany. The editions of Bärenreiter, Hal Leonard, Novello, Carl Fisher, Schirmer, CD sheet music, and "imslp.org" were utilized for the author's preparation of this text.

A brief history of the oratorio itself in the Baroque period, Handel's time, and in the Romantic period, Mendelssohn's time, is presented, and the original language of each oratorio aria noted. To enable the author to arrive at some viable interpretations of each aria, triangulation of data was used based on 1) What the text of the aria is saying; 2) What the character singing the aria is experiencing in context; and 3) What the composer intends for the given aria as evidenced by the music. The interpretation of an aria is considered valid when based on the agreement of two or all of the above criteria. To avoid interruptions in the narrative, these criteria have been incorporated holistically into the text.

2
Two Oratorio Composers

Handel as an English Oratorio Composer

George Frideric Handel was a composer who drew upon and amalgamated a number of musical resources (e.g., the operatic composition techniques of the day and the various musical styles of different nations) into his masterpieces. Moreover, his experiences and interactions with great musicians and scholars of his time contributed in no small way to his expertise and to his success. Handel, as an oratorio composer, was a fine melodist of vocal music and a master of musical drama. He combined everything he had learned from the diverse styles of other composers from different countries to create in due course a new dramatic work, the English oratorio. This featured the French style of the overture and the dance as well as the Italian style of *opera seria*, including the style of the aria and the achievement of dramatic effect. Abraham describes this amalgamation of various national "voices" as follows:

> Handel began as a German composer writing German music with an Italian accent, and developed into a cosmopolitan composer writing Italian music with a German command of solid technique and an occasional trace of English accent, caught mainly from Purcell.[1]

These musical skills, however, did not emerge at once but developed over time. Several aspects of Handel's education contributed to his development as a master of the later oratorio genre, one skill being his facility with language. With his ability to speak at least four languages reasonably fluently—German, French, Italian, and English—Handel was able to learn and develop a variety of European musical styles and idioms with ease. This was helped by the fact that he could also write in these four languages, which enabled him to speak and correspond with a variety of influential people, and indeed many luminaries of the day contributed to his musical education.[2]

As a young student, Handel "frequented the Gymnasium in Halle."[3] The Gymnasium was roughly the equivalent of an English Grammar School. It was also a Lutheran school, Mainwaring tells us, in which Handel learned the subjects needed to become an oratorio composer later: knowledge of the Bible and several languages (including Latin), music theory, and singing. While at the Gymnasium, Handel acquired a good grounding in Lutheran choral music, which quickly became the backbone of his choral music.

It was also in Halle that Handel received his first organ lessons as a young boy—between the ages of seven and nine, according to Victor Schoelcher (1804–1893), but possibly at the age of six, according to Mainwaring—from the young Friedrich Wilhelm Zachow, organist at the Halle parish church.[4] Under Zachow's tutelage, Handel learned the art of counterpoint, fugue, and canon, in which Zachow excelled. However, it was also from Zachow, Schoelcher reminds us, that Handel was introduced to a vast range of music in various genres and styles, including French elements of composition that Handel would encounter again during his Hamburg years. There were other musical pursuits, too, for it was during this time that Handel learned the violin and harpsichord, and even the oboe, which Schoelcher claims was Handel's favorite instrument at the time.[5] Again, these apprenticeships proved to be vital steps in improving Handel's appreciation of instruments other than keyboard ones, an appreciation that would stand him in good stead when composing his expanded orchestrations for later oratorios.

After his father's death in February 1697, Handel apparently continued to work as an assistant to Zachow in Halle, gaining much experience in composing organ pieces and (Lutheran) cantatas for church services. Moreover,

Zachow granted Handel access to his vast library of German and Italian music, which gave Handel a knowledge of various compositional forms that Zachow insisted he memorize by copying endless manuscripts by hand.[6]

Handel's academic education continued during this time at the University at Halle, where he matriculated in 1702.[7] There followed a one-year appointment as organist at the Calvinist *Domkirche* or Cathedral in Halle also in 1702. Around this time Handel developed a friendship with Georg Philipp Telemann, who was passing through Halle on his way to Leipzig, and with whom Handel had much in common. For example, both their families wanted them to practice law instead of pursuing a career in music. Both young men resisted, becoming instead important figures in the Baroque period. Telemann, unlike Handel, was self-taught, but this did not impair their mutual interest in exploring and analyzing melody, as well as in discussing the elements of fugue and counterpoint in the works of Johann Kuhnau, cantor of the *Thomaskirche* in Leipzig, and for whom Telemann acted as assistant. These exchanges, both in person and by correspondence, made a lasting impression on both Handel and Telemann, allowing Handel to develop both a theoretical and practical grounding in composing, for which he was quickly becoming renowned.

Handel's one-year probationary appointment at the *Domkirche* was not renewed, and by March 1703, the 19-year-old Handel had moved to Hamburg, where he met another prominent figure, the 22-year-old Johann Mattheson. The two became close friends, perhaps because they were "birds of a feather," and Mattheson, highly proficient in keyboard, violin, and composition, recognized those same skills in Handel. Handel's exposure to Italian music and opera were furthered in Hamburg, where he was employed, no doubt because of Mattheson's influence, as a second violinist in the orchestra of the Hamburg Opera, for which Mattheson also wrote several works. In fact, it was during the December 4, 1704, premiere of Mattheson's *Die Unglückliche Cleopatra* ("The Misfortune of Cleopatra") that he and Handel got into a potentially deadly fight, which has an emotional connection to the current study.

According to Predota, Mattheson had assigned the famous composer and conductor Reinhard Keiser to conduct the opera from the harpsichord, as was the custom.[8] Mattheson was playing the part of Marc Anthony in the opera and so had to be on stage. Unfortunately, Predota explains, Keiser "had a bit of a gambling and drinking problem" and left the performance halfway through to satisfy one or the other or both. Handel, to his credit, stepped in. However, when Mattheson returned after Act III and the glorious death of his character, he demanded to return to the harpsichord seat and take over the conducting. He saw this as his prerogative as the opera's composer, but Handel refused to leave the bench, and a terrible argument broke out right in the middle of the performance. Handel was already upset with Mattheson over the perceived stealing of one of Handel's potential pupils, Cyrill Wich, son of the British envoy to Hamburg, Sir John Wich, which certainly did not help the situation. Mattheson and Handel agreed to take the argument outside. The audience no doubt went with them. Swords were drawn. John Mainwaring, Handel's first biographer, reports his version of the outcome as follows:

> As they were coming out of the orchestra, he [Mattheson] made a push at him [Handel] with a sword, which, being aimed full at his heart, would for ever have removed him from the office he had usurped, but for the friendly score which he accidentally carried in his bosom; and through which to have forced it, would have demanded all the might of Ajax himself.[9]

The alternative ending, Predota claims, is that Mattheson's "push" was blocked, not by the full manuscript of *Cleopatra*, but by a large brass button on Handel's coat. Handel's life was spared, and the two young men were apparently soon reconciled. The relevance of the event to this study is that Handel was no stranger to the extreme emotions he wished to invoke in his audiences because he had experienced, on this occasion and at least one other, feelings of rage himself.

If Predota's version of the account is true, Keiser's irresponsible action in abandoning his post on this occasion probably served only to increase the rivalry that existed between himself and the young Handel.[10] Nevertheless, Handel certainly benefited from playing the violin for the Hamburg Opera, many performances of which came under Keiser's baton. During this period, Handel came to experience both the French-style overture and the German interpretation of Italian opera. Keiser was a composer of operas, too, so the existing rivalry may well have motivated Handel to compose his first two operas, *Almira* and *Nero,* in 1705, during this Hamburg period.

Italian was definitely the language of music in the Baroque era, especially in stage works, and Handel went to Italy the following year, 1706, to further his music studies and his knowledge of the language. Whether this was Handel's first or second visit is not clear, but we know he met substantial opera composers and teachers, such as Arcangelo Corelli, Alessandro Scarlatti, and Agostino Steffani. Under their influence, Handel flourished greatly, and his new operas were soon in demand. In Italy, Handel quickly learned operatic composition techniques as well as melodic ideas and new ways to expand the role of the orchestra, techniques used later in his oratorios. In Burrows' words,

> By contrast, although parallels may be drawn between the solo aria and a movement from a concerto featuring a solo instrument, Handel's orchestral music really forms a separate entity, related to the development of orchestral music in France and Italy in the period of Handel's youth.[11]

During Handel's Italian experience he came in contact with a new musical form, the oratorio. This form had grown mostly out of religious necessity in Italy. In papal circles, *opera seria* was considered vulgar, and some of its stars, the *castrati,* were considered an abomination, something God had not intended. The oratorio was the answer to the Church's complaints since it was a musical performance without costumes, scenery, or acting. Under these religious constraints, Handel was quite willing to learn this new form and learn he did from the works of one of the best, the famed Giacomo Carissimi, a foremost composer of Italian oratorios. Under the influence of Carrissimi's oratorios, Handel obliged his audience with a musical piece without staging or acting, namely his first oratorio, *La Resurrezione.* He may well have begun another, *Il Trionfo del Tempo e del Disinganno,* but the important thing for the current study is that Handel not only composed an oratorio, *La Resurrezione,* but also saw it performed in Rome—and to great acclaim. Handel now had a template, not merely for the oratorio form, but also for its public performance, both of which would guide him later during his years in London.

Ironically, when Handel arrived in London in 1710, after a brief period as *Kapellmeister* to the Elector of Hanover, he did not start writing oratorios, as one might expect, but Italian-style operas. There were good reasons for this. First of all, Italian opera was still relatively new to London audiences. Second, there were fewer restrictions on opera from the Church in England at this time. So, Handel immediately set to work on his first Italian opera composed in England, *Rinaldo*, first performed in London in 1711. It was an immediate success, and numerous operas followed.

Over the next twenty years, Handel continued to compose operas in the Italian language and style; however, it was an era that was slowly coming to an end. London audiences were growing tired of Italian operas sung by Italian singers and of not being able to understand exactly what was being sung, just as they were becoming bored with the mythological themes that had characterized Italian *opera seria* for so long. Consequently, when John Gay introduced his satirical *The Beggar's Opera* in January of 1728, London audiences were quite ready to hear familiar songs sung in English and did not mind poking fun at the nobility and at *opera seria* at the same time. The writing was on the wall.

Handel took note of the new trend, yet did not stop composing opera or instrumental works, often providing additional instrumental music to be performed between acts of his operas. He also inserted dance in the form of ballet, as he tried creative ways to retain his audiences, but the following years were difficult. In 1729, Handel became the co-manager of the Queen's Theatre in the Haymarket, which quickly proved to be a financial challenge as opera performances frequently ran at a loss owing to the aforementioned changing tastes of London audiences. The burden on Handel's shoulders was great:

> Market forces were crucial to Handel in his ventures addressed to the paying public, because his only regular income, from the court, was not enough to cover serious losses on them... In the course of his English career he took increasing responsibility for the management of his theater performances, to the extent of acting as his own impresario—hiring the theatre, singers, and orchestra, determining the method of ticket-buying...[12]

Moreover, the Italian singers whom Handel had brought back with him after a visit to Europe demanded, and usually received, extremely high fees. Loyalty, on the other hand, was often short-lived, and several of Handel's most accomplished singers left his company to join the rival *Opera of the Nobility*, formed in 1733 by aristocrats, such as the Prince of Wales, who were politically opposed to King George II. To make matters worse, the famous castrato Farinelli proved to be a star attraction, not in Handel's company, but rather in the competing *Opera of the Nobility*. These were indeed challenging times for Handel, with few guarantees. As Luckett puts it:

> Handel's position was precarious; it was certainly not as dire as some of his biographers, beginning with Burney, have claimed, but he lacked the security enjoyed by Bach at Leipzig or Telemann at Hamburg.[13]

Nevertheless, in the midst of these challenges, Handel was able to gain valuable experience that would contribute directly to his skill in composing the new genre of the English oratorio, namely facility with the English language itself. A 1732 revision of his earlier, *Esther,* originally performed privately in 1717 while Handel worked at Cannons, the Edgeware home of the Duke of Chandos, proved to be highly successful. It was initially composed to be a dramatic chamber piece with costumes and staging like an opera; however, the Bishop of London, Edmund Gibson, forbade the staging of any sacred work taken from the Bible. Handel complied, and so it was that circumstances turned *Esther* into the first English oratorio—as Burrows would say—by accident.[14]

Handel responded promptly to his subscribers' taste, and for the last twenty years of his life, composed about twenty English oratorios. As one commentator summed up Handel's progression from opera to oratorio:

> He composed with consummate skill in Italian or French forms and styles, and drew freely upon the German contrapuntal style and the English choral tradition. … After a brief stay as an organist at the cathedral of Halle (1702) while at the university there, he chose to make his career in opera, doing so at Hamburg (1703-6) and then in Italy (1706-10) at Florence, Rome, and Venice. In Italy, he encountered the leading genres of music and the leading composers of the age; Corelli, the two Scarlatti, Vivaldi, and Albinoni. Finally, after a brief time as Kapellmeister at the court of Hanover, Handel took up the challenge of Italian opera in London (1710-37). For years he directed his own opera companies until the London audience finally proved incapable of sustaining such ventures. From 1738, his efforts were primarily devoted to the composition and performance of his oratorios.[15]

It Is Enough!

In 1741 Handel's genius brought to fruition his most famous oratorio, *Messiah*. One could argue that it formed the culmination of every skill that Handel had developed over the long period of his musical training, for it contained an overture, solo arias, recitatives, a "Pastoral Symphony" as an interlude, and numerous majestic choruses. The dramatic element was ever present as well, residing in the powerful texts of the King James Version of the Bible.

Mendelssohn as an Oratorio Composer

Felix Mendelssohn-Bartholdy was born in 1809 into a wealthy family who enjoyed and supported the arts. Because of this, he received much support from his family and had no financial worries about daily living expenses. His father, Abraham Mendelssohn, was a banker, a well-educated man who loved the arts as did the rest of his family. Unfortunately, at that time, there was much hatred towards Jews in Germany. To protect his family, Abraham decided that they should convert to Christianity. Felix and his siblings (including his sister Fanny) were all baptized in 1816 into the Reformed Christian faith,[16] and Felix subsequently married Cécile Charlotte Sophie Jeanrenaud, the daughter of a French Reformed Church clergyman.

As a child, Felix Mendelssohn was a prodigy and spent his youth composing a variety of musical pieces: twelve string symphonies between the ages of 12 and 14; a piano quartet at age 13; a full orchestral symphony (Op. 11 in C Minor) and an opera, both at age 15; and a string octet and a new genre in the form of a "concert" overture, at age 16. However, the musical grounding that would contribute to these compositions and his later oratorios started almost a decade earlier. At age 6, he took piano lessons from his mother, continuing them at age 7 in Paris with Marie Bigot.[17] Plantinga also reports that "[Felix] received a systematic early training in music, beginning with lessons from his very talented mother."[18] More training in the rudiments of music followed under the influence of three highly accomplished musicians—Ludwig Berger (1777-1839), Eduard Rietz (1802-1832), and Carl Friedrich Zelter (1758-1832). Plantinga explains their contribution as follows:

> Born into a prominent Berlin Jewish family ... [Mendelssohn] had music lessons with the pianist Ludwig Berger and the violinist Eduard Rietz, who put him through a rigorous regime of figured bass, chorale harmonization, counterpoint, canon, and fugue. Zelter's

teaching followed North German traditions in musical instruction that derived from J. F. Kirnberger, F. W. Marpurg, and ultimately from their teacher, J. S. Bach. Mendelssohn thus received what was essentially an eighteenth-century musical education, and the extraordinary facility (and sometimes conservatism) of his music reflects this early training.[19]

A great influence on Mendelssohn's development as a composer was his sister Fanny, who, like her brother, was also a child prodigy. She probably composed around 500 pieces, including her first oratorio in 1831. Her works remained largely unknown until the late twentieth century, but her prodigious musical ability and the friendship she enjoyed with her more famous brother earned her the role of esteemed critic:

> The fact that from very early in their lives, and until Fanny's death (she died only six months before her brother), Felix would regularly submit his compositions to Fanny's discerning musical eye and ear, taking her critical advice to heart, and never hesitating to modify or excise entirely material that she found questionable. Felix began to refer to his older sister as "Minerva," the Roman goddess of wisdom, for her highly developed musical and intellectual insight.[20]

According to Todd,[21] Fanny was a great songwriter and an excellent pianist, and essentially better developed musically at an early age because of her parents' support in providing education at home for her and her siblings by hiring private tutors in music. As the two oldest children, Fanny and Felix always had music classes together, which gave Felix immediate access to Fanny's compositions. Indeed, her beautiful melodies must have influenced Felix when he composed the arias of his later oratorios, and he was always eager to listen to Fanny's comments and suggestions regarding all his compositions; his oratorio *Paulus* was no exception. Here Fanny was clearly protective of her younger brother's work—and certainly protective of her own adopted recommendations—for in addition to her critique, she made sure that musicians gave a faithful rendering of what she and her brother had written. Reich reports: "At his [Felix'] request, she [Fanny] wrote detailed critiques of his works and took his place at Berlin rehearsals of *Paulus* to assure a correct performance."[22]

The education of Felix and Fanny, along with their siblings, took place at home in Berlin with the distinguished private teachers mentioned previously. The children's homeschool subjects were music (piano and violin), literature, mathematics, foreign languages, arts (landscaping painting), and gymnastics along with dancing, swimming, and even horseback riding.[23] One can imagine that Mendelssohn's education was kept on a precise schedule under the observation and tight control of his parents, and not only his education but also the many social opportunities that were provided for him to meet important figures of the day at the Mendelssohns' home gatherings. Here Mendelssohn met famous philosophers, poets, and writers, one of whom was the famous German writer Johann Wolfgang von Goethe, for whom Mendelssohn frequently played, and it is well known that the two often visited each other. In fact, it was Goethe who encouraged Mendelssohn to visit Italy, which he did from 1830 to 1832.[24] As Todd remarks concerning Mendelssohn's education:

> In mathematics he was reading the fifth book of Euclid's *Elements* and with Fanny had lessons in history, arithmetic, geography, and German conversation. On Mondays and Tuesdays he attended the Singakademie, while twice a week Zelter came to the residence for lessons (around this time, as we have seen, Felix was beginning fugue in four parts). Finally there were two hours of violin lessons each week; Felix was now practicing etudes of Rodolphe Kreutzer, prized for their innovative extensions of left-hand technique… Music was at the center of the child's existence, but his studies also led him to delve into poetry.[25]

The Mendelssohn children's rigorous routine and musical support were obviously well known and something that Abraham Mendelssohn and his wife, Lea, proudly announced at their Sunday morning parties. Indeed, Robert Schumann mentions Mendelssohn's education and family support in a letter to his wife, Clara, in 1838, stating, "If I had grown up under circumstances similar to his, intended for music from childhood, I would surpass them all."[26] As a matter of fact, all this support and education prepared Mendelssohn to become one of the most important composers of the oratorio.

Not only did Mendelssohn devote himself to producing masterpieces, but also served as a conductor, editor, and educator. He founded a school of music in Leipzig, where he served as conductor of the Gewandhaus Orchestra. As an exceptionally talented music director there, he conducted not only his own works, but also pieces written by his contemporaries. Consequently, this position allowed him to experience various genres of music.

> He was one of Europe's busiest conductors, traveling ceaselessly between the major cities of Germany and England to present his own works and those of his revered predecessors, Haydn, Mozart, and Beethoven. Almost equally in demand as a pianist, he was a powerful exponent of the concertos of Mozart and Beethoven—and of Mendelssohn—as an antidote to the fashionable virtuoso keyboard music to be heard on all sides.[27]

Additionally, Mendelssohn edited Handel's oratorios for publication in England, though his edition was never published, and conducted his own arrangements of Handel's oratorios at several music festivals in both Germany and England. This immersion in Handel's oratorios could not help but influence him in the composition of his own two oratorios, *Paulus* (1836) and *Elijah* (1846), a point confirmed by German musicologist Hellmuth Christian Wolff:

> Mendelssohn took the subject of his E minor Fugue for piano, Op. 35, No. 1, from Handel's overture to *Semele*, and the arias *Jerusalem, die du tötest die Propheten* and *Gott sei mir gnädig* in *St. Paul*, as well as numerous other choruses in Mendelssohn's Psalm-cantatas, in the *Lobegesang*, and in *Elijah* (the final chorus of the first part) would be unthinkable without Handel's models.[28]

In 1828, at the age of only 19, Mendelssohn prepared his first edition of Handel's works, which included *Acis and Galatea* along with Handel's *Dettingen Te Deum*; both were performed in Berlin in the same year by the Singakademie. It is clear that Mendelssohn's interest in Handel's oratorios lies in their performance, for he was always mindful of what instruments may or may not have been available, perhaps because as a conductor, he had often experienced those situations himself where an instrument, e.g., an organ, was not at hand. Wolff offers valuable insight:

> *Israel in Egypt* became Mendelssohn's favorite oratorio. He directed an additional performance of the entire second part at a concert in Düsseldorf... At the same time Mendelssohn edited the original version of *Israel in Egypt* for the London Handel Society. His preface,

written in English, is dated July 4, 1844. In October 1835 Mendelssohn had received the 32 volumes of the English Handel edition (published by Arnold) as a gift from the Cologne Music Festival Committee… For these reasons Mendelssohn espoused the publication of some original Handel scores in Germany; to facilitate performances the *bass continuo* was to be realized… Mendelssohn offered to write the organ part, which was to serve as *basso continuo*, for the full-score editions; he also offered to arrange that part for wind instruments in order to make performances without organ possible, thus revealing an exceedingly practical attitude.[29]

With regard to the musical style and idiom of the oratorio, comprising recitatives, arias, and choruses, it is true that Mendelssohn was immensely influenced by Handel, but he was also greatly influenced by Bach. In 1829, the then 20-year-old Mendelssohn revived Bach's *St. Matthew Passion* and publicly performed it in the same year in Berlin, which gave him experience of how Bach treated choral interludes, thus influencing his own interpretation of chorales:

> During Mendelssohn's first years in Leipzig the composition of his that attracted the most attention in Germany was his oratorio *St. Paul*, completed in 1836… All essentials of the Handelian oratorio—accompanied and unaccompanied recitative, aria, and both homophonic and fugal choruses—are present here. In addition, at many points Mendelssohn introduces chorales, harmonized approximately in the style of Bach, as reflective commentary upon the drama.[30]

However, Mendelssohn injected his own genius and lyricism into *St. Paul*, reflecting earlier lessons in melody from his sister Fanny's works as well as from his own *Songs without Words*, published a good five years before *St. Paul*. In this way, Mendelssohn was able to truly usher in the new era of musical romanticism:

> In effect, Felix's oratorio offered a blend of historicism and contemporary musical idioms, of baroque chorales and fugues with modern orchestration suffused with a Lied-like lyricism, that popularized the complexities and severities of Bach and Handel for a newly empowered, middle-class musical culture.[31]

As far as the operatic genre was concerned, Mendelssohn was less successful. Although he composed three German operas, or *Singspiele, Die Heimkehr aus der Fremde, Die beiden Neffen, Die Hochzeit des Camacho*, his operas never succeeded as Handel's had done. A fourth attempt, namely to compose the opera *Loreley*, in 1846, was never completed, as his health deteriorated rapidly after his sister Fanny died. In fact, they both died in 1847—Fanny in May and Felix in November. Ironically, Mendelssohn endeavored throughout his life to seek a suitable libretto for an opera, but for some reason, he could not make that happen.

> [Felix Mendelssohn] also attempted opera without much success. The only opera by Mendelssohn to receive a public production in his lifetime was *Die Hochzeit des Camacho* (1827), fashioned from a tale from Cervantes' *Don Quixote*. Its success, however, was limited; after a few performances at Berlin, it was withdrawn... Left unfinished was his large opera, *Die Loreley*.[32]

According to Eatock, "If Mendelssohn's life had not been cut short at the age of 38, there is every reason to believe that he would have completed *Die Loreley*—and if the opera had been a success, the story of Mendelssohn's relationship with the lyric stage would have been cast in an entirely different light."[33]

Todd also reports on Mendelssohn's attempt at this large-scale vocal oeuvre:

> For the rest of his life Mendelssohn continued to search for a suitable opera libretto, but rejected dozens of proposals from poets and playwrights, including Karl von Holtei, J. R. Planché (the librettist of Weber's *Oberon*), Karl Immermann, Eugène Scribe and Helminie von Chézy (the librettist of Weber's *Euryanthe*), and from his friends Klingemann, Ludwig Robert and Devrient (Devrient lamented his friend's 'operatic destiny' as a 'Hamlet-like tragedy') ... Finally, in 1845 Mendelssohn took up the Lorelei legend and began an extended collaboration with Emanuel Geibel on an opera in three acts, with continuous music. But the composer lived long enough only to begin the music for the first act, of which the finale and two short numbers were issued posthumously.[34]

Mendelssohn, however, did leave a legacy of two large-scale oratorios, *Elijah*, Op. 70 (1846), which has become one of the most frequently performed nineteenth-century choral works, since it was composed as a concert piece and has sometimes been staged as well, and the earlier oratorio, *Paulus*, Op. 36, in 1836.

Even though Felix Mendelssohn was a composer in the Romantic period, his oratorios were certainly influenced by George Frideric Handel from the Baroque period. In his 1959 article titled "Mendelssohn and Handel," Wolff confirms the influence that Handel had on Mendelssohn's music. Indeed, Mendelssohn endeavored to emulate Handel's oratorios in his own compositions, an activity no doubt facilitated by his professional preoccupation with both editing and conducting Handel's originals. It is not surprising, therefore, that Mendelssohn interjected many of Handel's techniques and musical idioms into his own oratorios. In defense of this practice, some researchers (e.g., John Winemiller, Sedley Taylor, Winton Dean, and John Roberts) have argued that Handel's music itself contained borrowed musical fragments and ideas from his teachers and predecessors (e.g., Reinhart Keiser, Georg Philipp Telemann, Alessandro Stradella, Alessandro Scarlatti, Giacomo Carissimi, Giovanni Bononcini, and Gottlieb Muffat, among others), including self-borrowings, and that this borrowed music became fundamental in Handel's creation of his own musical works. It can be argued, therefore, that Mendelssohn, by applying Handel's musical forms to his own compositions, similarly utilized his own genius and created masterpieces, admittedly based on pre-existing music even before Handel's time, but making it distinctly his own.

In conclusion, Mendelssohn's major contribution to the genre of the oratorio are the two excellent compositions mentioned above—*Paulus* (*St. Paul*) and *Elijah*—which became part of the standard oratorio repertoire, and the introduction of his version of Handel's oratorios to London audiences. Without this latter endeavor, the publication of Handel's complete works by Friedrich Chrysander from 1858 to 1894 would have been greatly delayed.

3

The Oratorio in the Baroque and Romantic Periods

There are similarities in the oratorios of the Baroque and Romantic periods. Handel, thanks to his training and experience in Italy, established the form of the oratorio that Mendelssohn was to study and build upon later. However, there were differences, too, and, as will be seen, Mendelssohn developed his own melodies and adapted the earlier forms to create a synthesis of the Baroque and Romantic styles.

The Oratorio in the Baroque Period: Handel

Although the year 1685 was not the beginning of the Baroque period, it was, nevertheless, the beginning of what was to become the zenith of the Baroque period and was, therefore, an important year in western music history. Indeed, the year marked the birth of many prominent composers: Handel in February of 1685, almost forty years after the Thirty Years War ended, in Halle, Germany; Johann Sebastian Bach in March, in Eisenach, Germany, nearly a month after Handel's birth; and John Gay, composer of highly popular *The Beggar's Opera*, in June of the same year in Barnstaple, England. The Thirty Years War (1618-1648), a dramatic consequence of Luther's Reformation of 1517, is also relevant to the development of the Baroque period, for Luther himself was also a composer of hymns and choral music. In fact, it was Luther's compositions that formed much of the music syllabus of the Halle Gymnasium where Handel studied and which influenced him later in the composing of his English oratorios. In the context of the Thirty Years War, it was the Peace of Westphalia treaties, signed between May and October of 1648, that gave religious autonomy to individual states in Germany—and indeed throughout Europe—thus granting the Halle Gymnasium the legal right to have a Lutheran syllabus.

The Baroque period of theorists and composers commented on and produced many musical forms that would stimulate human emotion, including the genres of cantata, opera, oratorio, and sonata, each relying on previous theories of harmony. However, a fundamental change in harmony occurred during the Baroque period, as reliance on modal systems of the past gradually yielded to the major-minor system of tonal relationships. This chord-based or chordal nature of harmony was reflected in the figured bass, indicating which notes should comprise the accompanying harmonies. Perhaps the most notable change of style was the shift to a new kind of texture: A typical Baroque piece consisted of a mellifluous melodic line and an anchoring bass line. This polarity between the melody and the bass resulted in an apparent indifference to the inner parts, as evidenced in the system of notation called *basso continuo*, above which the other continuo players were required to fill in the notes *ad libitum*.[35] Through the *basso continuo*, a characteristic feature of most Baroque forms, music developed from counterpoint, the intertwining of two or more separate melodic lines, to homophony, which comprised a strong melody line supported by—rather than competing with—other lines based on chords, thus changing the music structure from linear-melodic to chordal-harmonic.

In addition to the above influences, the Baroque period also gave rise to the concept of the "doctrine of the affections,"[36] based on the belief that music moved the audience's emotions and tried to deliver the composer's intended feelings primarily through the words of a song, with music as their persuasive vehicle. According to Hill, Emeritus Professor of Musicology at the University of Illinois, Urbana-Champaign, the eighteenth-century music theorist and composer Johann Georg Neidhardt wrote in 1706: "The purpose of music is to stimulate all the affections."[37] For some, this was just the beginning, an important stepping-stone toward a higher purpose, indeed one that pushed audiences towards the moral and ethical high ground and invited them to become their better selves. Handel may well have heard this idea from his friend Johann Mattheson, for Hill cites the latter as claiming: "Where there is no passion, no affect to be found, there is also no virtue."[38]

There were specific musical forms that helped produce the affections that would ideally lead audiences to virtuous action. Generally, a single piece of music attempted to express a single affection. As it happened, among the various affections that Baroque composers were interested in were the more violent and dramatic ones. This new interest was accompanied by the development of a new style, the *stile moderno*, which comprised not only the previously mentioned figured bass, but also a new way of looking at the melodic line, in a form referred to as *monody*. The early 1600s saw some of the most radical experiments in the representation of the affections which helped shape monody, and in turn became recognizable generally as a solo song with instrumental accompaniment. Behind the development of monody, there was a belief that the text should govern the music, as opposed to the Renaissance belief that the music should govern the text. The oratorio recitative, in particular, reflected this belief, since it was considered a dramatic monody during this period. It attempted to imitate speech, and to this end, its rhythmic pace was freely declamatory, closely following the accentual patterns of the text. Therefore, the old rules of counterpoint were often broken, and dissonances—also part of the *stile moderno*—were used more freely to express the text more effectively.

This importance of "words over music," or the determination not to sacrifice meaning to music, had at least some of its roots in Italy and in the works of Giacomo Carissimi, from whose manuscripts Handel mostly likely gleaned valuable oratorio models. Roger Ardrey, in his doctoral dissertation tracing the influence of Carissimi's Latin sacred works on the Biblical oratorios of Handel, expresses a certain confidence that Handel somehow came into contact with Carissimi's works:

> What authoritative material there is will be used to find whether Handel had knowledge of or came into contact with Carissimi's manuscripts in the St. Apollinare Chapel in Rome. Of course, this does not eliminate the possibility that Handel may have had contact with some of Carissimi's compositions through performances of his music or from seeing some of Carissimi's work copied by someone else.[39]

Carissimi subscribed to the "Affektenlehre" of the period and was a master at combining words and music, but he was also responsible for going beyond purely Christian doctrinal texts in Latin; he sensed that words could also tell stories that reflected the vagaries and spiritual challenges of the human condition. In other words, in Carissimi's new oratorio form, the libretto was no longer a sermon, but rather a play. As Ardrey explains, "The element of drama was one of Carissimi's strong artistic characteristics. The manner in which he expressed feelings through music demonstrated that Carissimi was a typical example of an early Baroque dramatist who subscribed to the 'doctrine of the affections.'"[40]

This reconceptualizing of the oratorio as a dramatic piece, rather than a liturgical composition, affected all the singers, particularly the chorus. No longer did the chorus play a narrative role, acting as a commentator explaining elements of the drama for the benefit of the audience—as was the case in the chorus's Greek literary origins—but it was now a salient part of the drama itself. When Handel visited Italy from 1706 to 1710, Carissimi had been deceased for eleven years, but it is almost certain, as Ardrey points out, that his manuscripts were available in one form or another. Also, one of Carissimi's students, Alessandro Scarlatti, may well have made copies of his teacher's works and shown them to Handel. So, it was probable, Ardrey continues, that "Handel might have learned effective uses of the dramatic structured chorus from Carissimi. Carissimi accepted the chorus as a medium representing people—a congregation composed of human beings expressing basic human emotions."[41] This new role of the chorus, then, was the same as it was for the soloists, namely to express emotions that would move the audience towards a moral ideal.

Some of the musical elements that would express the more extreme emotion of anger were inherited from Carissimi's fellow countryman, Claudio Monteverdi, who was his contemporary for almost the first forty years of Carissimi's life. Monteverdi used specific musical devices to portray specific moods. According to Carter, these comprised arpeggios to denote conflict in general and the *stile concitato* to portray anger.[42] The *stile concitato*, or *genere concitato*, as Monteverdi called it, which translates approximately as "animated style," comprised the rapid repetition of notes and sustained trills to express extreme emotion. Carissimi demonstrated this style in his oratorio *Jephte*, as Ardrey notes:

30

The subject of Jephta [was] set to music as early as 1650 by Carissimi and later by Handel, "who surely must have known Carissimi's works." This expressive dramatic style is especially noticeable through Carissimi's use of the "stile concitato" found in the early portions of Jephta.[43]

Handel's use of his many resources was not, however, composition by rote. As a genius of stage work, Handel knew how to vary the use of choruses, as exemplified in his most celebrated oratorio, *Messiah*. Here choruses frequently follow arias as they had for his friend Mattheson, an example of which can be found in Mattheson's 1716 oratorio, *Die gnädige Sendung Gottes des Heiligen Geistes*. However, Handel did not feel bound by this sequence. Of the first five pieces of Part II of *Messiah*, for instance, four of them are choruses, with rich orchestral accompaniments. What is more, if Handel wanted to write counterpoint, he did. Poultney provides an admirable summary of Handel's contributions to the oratorio genre:

Latin oratorio readily assimilated monody, but perhaps because of its roots in the motet, it did not remain significant in Italy after the early masterpieces by Giacomo Carissimi. Oratorio reached its peak in the late Baroque work of Handel. Having mastered Italian oratorio and opera, he created English oratorios as a Protestant entertainment of dramatic nature. Much of the power of the Handelian oratorio stems from the composer's expansion of regular operatic resources by the addition of choral numbers, contrapuntal writing, and an increased role for the orchestra.[44]

As one might expect, the list of oratorio resources is more extensive than indicated above. Ornamentation, for instance, was one of the principal Baroque vehicles that allowed performers to express human emotion with greater freedom of interpretation. Although Handel determined the melodic style of arias based on affection, he left room for performers to ornament the melody according to what they felt at the time of the performance. In other words, through ornamentation, Baroque music allowed a significant amount of spontaneity and improvisation that went beyond the notes of the written score.

Another important influence on Handel by his predecessors was in the realm

31

of instrumentation. Handel already heard and experienced the German Protestant oratorios in Hamburg, where Keiser's use of an unusual instrument, a huge bell called a "carillon," in his oratorio *Saul* obviously impressed him, for in *Der Siegende David* ("The Victorious David"), Handel employed this instrument in the same situation, namely when the chorus praises David's victorious march. The triumphant sound of the bell, along with the exultant singing of the choir, provokes King Saul to anger and jealousy and fills his aria—"What do I here?"—with extreme emotion.

Mattheson's influence on Handel appears again in Handel's English oratorio *Athalia*, featuring the *non-da capo* ("no repeat from the beginning") aria, which broke the tradition of the *da capo* ("from the beginning") "ABA" form, where the final section was a reprise of the first, usually with some ornamentation. Handel's friend Telemann also produced several oratorios in Hamburg between 1722 and 1767, and through correspondence with his friend, Handel may well have been familiar with most, if not all, of them. Hill emphasizes the influence of the Hamburg oratorio on Handel's style as follows:

> The obvious precedent for this [Handel's English oratorio] is, of course, the Hamburg oratorio as exemplified in the works of Reinhard Keiser, Handel's mentor, and Mattheson and Telemann, his two closest friends during his early years and throughout his life. Passages from two of Telemann's cantatas printed at Hamburg in 1725-26 turn up in Handel's *Messiah* (1742) and *Solomon* (1749).[45]

To summarize, Handel mastered not only compositional techniques of Italian opera and of the Hamburg oratorio tradition, but also the art of adaptation, since he seemed to instinctively know how to efficiently and impressively compose arias that would appeal to the changing tastes of London audiences. Handel did not create the oratorio form *per se*, yet his talent and his financially demanding milieu, as mentioned above in Chapter 2, together led him to become a pioneer of a new musical drama, one that would become known as the English oratorio. Indeed, for the last twenty years of his life, Handel composed around twenty such oratorios.

In answer to the question as to how Handel managed to produce so much in so short a time, we return to the principles of borrowing and repeating, neither of which were considered a crime, as they might be today. On the contrary, they were more of a practical necessity, given the time constraints and pressures under which Handel and other composers worked. It must be remembered that there were no recording devices in Handel's day, and audiences had to rely on their musical memories, which they did not mind having refreshed by repeat performances of works—in whole or in part. In addition, longer pieces, such as oratorios, could be prolonged further by the insertion of melodies and forms from previous works. One such form was the anthem, a celebratory and inspiring piece with the text usually based on scripture or liturgy and often consisting of several movements, the borrowing of which would be a useful way to lengthen a piece that needed to last perhaps two or three hours. Smith explains how Handel used certain anthems to complement his oratorios:

> Some of his oratorios to varying degrees incorporated music, and sometimes words, of his anthems: two of his Coronation Anthems appeared in his public version of *Esther*, two Coronation Anthems and four Chandon Anthems in *Deborah* and a Chandos Anthem in *Athalia*; the first act of *Israel in Egypt* took over the funeral anthem for Queen Caroline, after this had been considered and rejected as the elegy for *Saul*; *Belshazzar* used two Chandos Anthems ... and the *Occasional Oratorio* a Coronation Anthem... Artistic consideration aside, Handel had excellent marketing reasons for absorbing his anthems and his anthem style into his oratorios: the public loved them.[46]

Handel was not the only English composer interested in the concept and form of the sacred dramatic dialogue. Indeed, from the early years of the seventeenth century, several English composers had written sacred dialogues, one of the earliest being John Hilton's *The Dialogue of Job, God, Satan, Job's Wife, and the Messengers*, "possibly composed as early as 1616," *Grove Music Online* reports. Some composers used the verse anthem form, as did Richard Portman in his 1635 piece *How Many Hired Servants*, based on the Biblical story of The Prodigal Son, where the verses contained the dialogue and the chorus the narrative. Of those composers whose works we know, Henry Blowman, Benjamin Lamb, Nicolas Lanier, Henry Purcell, Robert Ramsey, and John Wilson, all composed in the dramatic dialogue form, but the form went undeveloped in England. Smither reports:

Thus English composers made a tentative beginning with the

type of composition that might have led to a fully developed oratorio, perhaps by way of a dramatic verse anthem; they did not carry on this development, however, and when Handel arrived in England he found audiences that were unfamiliar with the form.[47]

The unfamiliarity of London audiences with the oratorio form that Handel had learned in Europe worked to his advantage, for once he arrived in London in 1710, he was able to stamp his own mark on it. Smither explains,

> When Handel arrived in England, he found audiences that were totally unfamiliar with the oratorio. The English oratorio is Handel's creation, his remarkable synthesis of elements derived from a variety of sources: the Italian *opera seria* and *oratorio volgare*, the choral style exhibited in his Latin psalms composed during his Italian period, the German oratorio, the French classical drama, the English masque, and English choral music.[48]

Oratorios based on the Old Testament pleased the audiences of London much more than did the *opera seria* plots based on Greek epic stories via Italy, which sounded unfamiliar to Handel's audiences. On the other hand, stories from the Old Testament and the Apocrypha invited English audiences to identify themselves as the Israelites of the day, the idea of people chosen by God, a nation set on defending the Kingdom—and the Empire—with fortitude and fidelity. However, Handel faced a significant problem regarding the language of his compositions: although his English singers could manage English texts with relative ease, they lacked both the language and the vocal technique to equal that of Italian opera singers, as Ruth Smith describes:

> English singers were unable to sing such elaborate music as he wanted to compose; only Italian singers had the technique for what was currently the most complex solo vocal music being written ... But the Italians could not sing English convincingly. On the other hand there were no English singers available who had the theatrical talent for the parts he enjoyed writing for male leads.[49]

Handel also employed the technique of word painting in his oratorios, which will be presented more in depth in Chapter 4.

Like opera, the oratorio is composed of several elements: soloists who sing the roles of dramatic characters, an ensemble or a choir to sing choruses (including *turba*[50]), an orchestra, and sometimes a narrator, with the main forms being arias, recitatives, and choruses. Unlike operas of the day, however, oratorios used mostly sacred themes as "sermons" to encourage moral rectitude, whereas operas were more likely to use stories from Greek tragedies to purge the emotions. Even so, the two forms often overlapped with regard to their dramatic nature and musical forms. Poultney summarizes the Baroque Oratorio and Handel's contribution to the genre as follows:

> Oratorio began as a part of extra-liturgical religious services in Roman prayer halls (oratories), where it served partly to entice music-lovers back into the Counter-Reformation fold. From their beginnings in the Lauda and the spiritual dialogue, oratorio in both Italian (*oratorio volgare*) and Latin (*oratorio latino*) flourished in Italy and in such Italian musical cities as Vienna, but after about 1650 it drew even closer to opera… Like opera, oratorio spread from Italy across Europe but, apparently because of its religious purpose, vernacular languages and a more conservative style were generally adhered to, and native composers played a larger role in its history… Although he embraced a wider range of subjects and types than did the Italians, Handel's oratorios generally reflect a truly Italian dramatic character and actually constitute religious or simply moral entertainments not designed for church performance. Because of his complete mastery of Italian opera and acquaintance with the English masque and the German Protestant oratorio, his enhanced choral and orchestral resources, and his remarkable musical and dramatic gifts, Handel's oratorios represent perhaps even better than opera the quintessential values of Baroque sung drama.[51]

As previously mentioned in Chapter 2, Handel not only composed a concert's main event, the oratorio, but also provided music to be played between the acts. Handel was a master of the keyboard and an organist with a virtuoso talent for improvisation, which enabled him to take advantage of the two musical interludes between his three-act oratorios by playing his own compositions. As Smith puts it, "Handel made his skill as an organist literally a central feature of his oratorio performances from 1735 until the end of his active life, by performing his own organ concertos between the acts. If we wish to consider the nature of Handelian oratorio as Handel devised it and his own audiences heard it, we should not neglect this vital component."[52]

To summarize, Handel's compositional style embraced the borrowed musical ideas and elements from his own works and from those of his teachers, as well as from other composers that he met on his travels. This gave him a storehouse of new styles, more freedom of interpretation by use of ornamentation, plus borrowed instrumentation, and forms taken from his anthems and psalms. This borrowing, it can be argued, assisted him greatly in offering his audiences beautiful melodic lines and in unveiling another level—some would say genre—of musical drama: the English oratorio. However, in the end, the masterful stamp he placed on his oratorios was all his own.

The Oratorio in the Romantic Period: Mendelssohn

Whereas Handel's later years in London saw the heyday of the English oratorio genre, Mendelssohn's early years in new nineteenth-century Germany ushered in a *revival* of the music of the Baroque period, with an emphasis on Handel's oratorios. Mendelssohn endeavored to create a Romantic period-styled oratorio based on the music of his predecessors, particularly Handel and Bach. As mentioned in Chapter 2, oratorios in the Baroque era were performed both in theatres and in churches, without acting, costumes, or scenery—and they were only performed during Lent. Even so, church authorities in both Germany and Italy banned any secular-themed opera performances, such as those of *opera seria*, in buildings they considered to be sacred. However, in the so-called Romantic era of the nineteenth century, performance restrictions based on time and place were lifted, which meant that sacred oratorios did not have to take place solely in churches but could also be performed in theatres. Ironically, this changed the role of churches as they began to compete more with theatres as places of entertainment.

As mentioned earlier, the purpose of composing an opera-like sacred work, the oratorio, in the vernacular was to reach a larger audience and edify people, inspiring them towards more moral behavior. Although the text was based on the Bible, the sacred oratorio actually played no part in the worship service itself. Unfortunately, one could only categorize an oratorio as "church music" insofar as it used a "church text" and was actually performed inside a church, but it was often seen merely as pious entertainment, rather than spiritual edification through music. Even though it was based on Judeo-Christian stories from Scripture, the oratorio was now being performed mainly outside of churches and on the same level as secular entertainment, not as a basis for experiencing liturgy, moral teaching, or worship. Only in Italy had the oratorio originally functioned as part of worship services during the Baroque period. By the 1830s, oratorios were being performed more frequently in theatres than in sanctuaries. Even so, it was hoped that this musical form could still serve as a moral teaching tool.

During the Romantic period throughout Europe, oratorios developed into the specialized territory of the choral communities that consisted of mostly amateur musicians, as oratorios began to be featured more prominently in many music festivals as part of a regular repertoire. Typically, Germany and England held regular festivals, and many composers, including Mendelssohn, composed oratorios for them, rather than for church performances. The Lower Rhine Music Festival in Düsseldorf, Germany, for example, was one of the leading music festivals[53] of the day, and it was here that Mendelssohn's own works were also featured, his oratorio *Paulus* having its premiere on the evening of Whitsunday, May 22, 1836.[54] His *Elijah* was first showcased in England, in the Birmingham Musical Festival, which took place on Wednesday morning, August 26, 1846.[55] Both occasions involved many choral associations, consisting of amateur members mostly, and were performances on a grand scale. Edwards reports in *The Musical Times* how many musicians participated in the premiere of *Paulus*:

> In addition to "St. Paul," there were performed Beethoven's Choral Symphony, and his Overtures … The performance took place in the Rittersaal, "but the room," says Hiller, "was too small for the large audience and orchestra"… The orchestra (led by Ferdinand David) consisted of 172 players; the chorus numbered 364, a total of 536 performers. The chorus was thus distributed: 106 sopranos, 60 altos, 90 tenors, and 108 basses. All the singers, with the exception of the soloists, were amateurs, as were also the greater part of the band. It was this circumstance that gave to the Festival one interesting characteristic.[56]

Also, Smither comments on Mendelssohn's two oratorios:

> Oratorio subjects that had long been traditional in Germany, particularly those using biblical stories, continued to be popular in the 19th century. The increasing interest in the oratorios of Handel in the first half of the 19th century contributed to the popularity of biblical oratorios, particularly those based on Old Testament stories… Mendelssohn's *Paulus* ('St Paul', 1836) and *Elijah* ('Elias', 1846) both based on scriptural texts, also represent the traditional tendency in

librettos; both were extremely popular works in their time, and *Elijah*, first performed in Birmingham, England, has retained its popularity to the present day in both English- and German-speaking areas.[57]

In addition to his two large-scale oratorios, *Paulus* and *Elijah*, Mendelssohn also conducted his own edition of Handel's oratorios at the same music festivals. In Düsseldorf, as the director of the Lower Rhine Music Festivals, he also conducted oratorios by Bach and Haydn, in addition to those of Handel, including works such as *Messiah, Israel in Egypt, Judas Maccabaeus, Samson, Alexander's Feast, Saul, Die Schöpfung, Die Jahreszeiten,* and *Du Hirte Israel.* Indeed, Mendelssohn's passion and love for the older composers can be seen in his repertoire. According to Smither,

> Typical of festivals, the centerpiece was virtually always an oratorio: Handel dominated—increasingly so as the century wore on and the Handel revival gained momentum—and Haydn's *Schöpfung* and *Jahreszeiten* were also standard... Despite the Handelian emphasis, however, many nineteenth-century oratorios were also heard, the most famous of which were Mendelssohn's *Paulus* (premier under the composer in Düsseldorf, 1836), and *Elias* (performed in Düsseldorf, 1863).[58]

Smither notes how the Romantic period oratorios were performed in Germany and England, and what distinct aspects were carried over from earlier periods.

> In Germany—
> The music of the 19th-century German oratorio, like the libretto, reveals a mixture of traditional and new procedures. Traditional for Germany is the use of the chorale and the emphasis on the chorus, but the performing forces tended to be far greater than in the 18th century. With the growing emphasis on performances of oratorios at music festivals in 19th-century Germany and the period's penchant for massive performances, the composer with a festival performance in mind could expect several hundred voices in his chorus. The aspects of German musical Romanticism that are new in the oratorio of the period are essentially those of German musical Romanticism in general, and particularly of Romantic opera: the large, colourful orchestra, new harmonic and melodic styles and new approaches to motivic and structural unification.[59]

In England—
The history of oratorio in 19th-century England is inseparable from that of the provincial music festivals, which were the chief institutions to cultivate oratorio composition and performance. Of particular importance is the Three Choirs Festival, which continued in the early 19th century to emphasize Handel's works. The festivals of Birmingham and Leeds were also of special importance for the history of the oratorio. In the first half of the 19th-century selections from and at times complete performances of the oratorios of foreign composers began to appear on English programmes. Among the more popular works of foreign composers were Haydn's *Creation*; Spohr's *Calvary* (i.e. *Des Heilands letzte Stunden*, first performed in London, 1837) and *The Fall of Babylon* (composed for the Norwich Festival of 1842); and Mendelssohn's *St Paul* (performed at Liverpool in 1836, for the first time in England, and conducted by the composer at the Birmingham Festival of 1837) and *Elijah* (first performed at the Birmingham Festival of 1846, conducted by the composer).[60]

What changed the accessibility of music in general in the nineteenth century was the growth of the middle-class. Following on the heels of the French Revolution came the so-called Industrial Revolution, which began in England in the latter half of the eighteenth century and quickly spread thereafter to Europe. It impacted the everyday life of citizens of every nation, as hand-crafted goods gave way to machine-produced ones and industry moved out of the home to the factory. Mass production was now the order of the day, and lower prices made products more affordable to more people— and there were more jobs created by the need to keep factories running, resulting in more disposable income to those not of the aristocracy. Thus the middle class was born, with their new-found wealth spilling over into the realms of music, for now more people were able and willing to buy tickets to music festivals, and classical music performances were able to reach more audiences than ever before. During the Baroque period, most composers' livelihoods had relied on the patronage of the aristocracy, and composers wrote music-on-demand at the request of their patrons, music for private occasions such as weddings, funerals, parties, coronations, and so forth. However, the Romantic-period composers of the nineteenth century wrote their music for music festivals and public concerts, which now middle-class audiences were eager to attend.

4

Handel's Oratorio Arias from a Performer's Perspective

Before analyzing each aria in detail prior to a performance, a singer must learn how to prepare what is referred to as "the singer's body" in order to initiate the resonant sound necessary to perform an oratorio aria—or any song for that matter—in an effective and aesthetically pleasing way. It means that the body must be ready both physically and mentally. To accomplish this, the singer must adopt good posture, take in a sufficient amount of air through the mouth or nose, open the throat as if beginning to yawn, relax the jaw, and release any tension before taking an inhalation of air. The singer should take care not to let the shoulders or upper chest elevate during the inhalation process. Dr. Karen Tillotson Bauer, a specialist in voice pedagogy, suggests that good posture for singing entails standing tall and keeping the body well aligned. A singer can usually achieve this by standing against a wall and making sure that the head, upper back, and buttocks touch it. In her book, *The Essentials of Beautiful Singing,* Bauer encourages students to practice the tried and tested principles of singing that she has taught for more than 30 years at North Park University, IL. Her method is based on a three-step mantra she refers to as "OOFing":

1) Opening the Body (breath management);
2) Opening the Throat (resonance); and
3) "Forwarding" the Articulation (enunciation).

This three-step technique can serve as an essential checklist for singing and functions well when everything works together as one system.

As mentioned in the "Methodology" section in Chapter 1, the text of each oratorio aria, whether or not the text is based on exact words from Scripture or paraphrased, will be presented. The original key(s) of each aria, as well as the *tessitura*, tempo, character's role, librettist, musical form, style, meter, orchestration, tonal structure, and some vocal techniques will also be discussed. In order to provide suggestions for viable—and reliable—interpretations of each aria, the methodology for analyzing each song, as mentioned in Chapter 1, will be based on the triangulation of data from three categories: 1) What the text of the aria is saying; 2) What the character singing the aria is experiencing in context; and 3) What the composer intends for the given aria as evidenced by the music.

ᘓ

"What Do I Hear? ... To Him Ten Thousands!" and "With Rage I Shall Burst, His Praises to Hear!"
from *Saul* by G. F. Handel

These two arias, "What Do I Hear? ... To Him Ten Thousands!" and "With Rage I Shall Burst, His Praises to Hear!" can be classified as "rage and envy" arias, sung by the character Saul, the first king of Israel, who was ordained by the prophet Samuel, and who eventually does wrong in the eyes of the Lord.

Handel's *Saul* premiered at the King's Theatre in London in 1739, and he revised it several times for subsequent performances. During this time, Handel was about to cease composing *opera seria* owing to insufficient subscriptions to his 1738 opera season.[61] This situation led Handel to compose his oratorio *Saul* since he knew this genre appealed to London audiences. These two arias occur in Scene 3 of Act I, Nos. 23-26 and take approximately two minutes and thirty seconds to perform. They are comprised of an *accompagnato* recitative ("What do I hear?" – No. 22), a brief chorus in celebration of David's victory over the Philistines ("David his ten thousands slew, Ten thousand praises are his due" – No. 24), and another *accompagnato* recitative ("To Him ten thousands!" – No. 25) which is followed by an aria ("With rage I shall burst" – No. 26). Interestingly, before the recitative, "What Do I Hear?," the women's chorus showers more praise on David than on King Saul (for it is David rather than Saul who is the source of the women's joy), as the chorus welcomes the two together as they march into Jerusalem to celebrate their victory. This is a double-edged sword for Saul in his precarious mental state: not only is his military prowess undermined by the unfavorable numbers in the chorus, but also his manliness is undermined by the fact that it is the women folk who show such adulation for David. This double insult exacerbates Saul's madness even further.

The result is that Saul does evil in the sight of the Lord by murderously pursuing David, since Saul madly covets David's success in battle. As mentioned previously in Chapter 2, Handel uses the kettle drum to emphasize David's triumphs, just as Keiser had used the same instrument for the same purpose in his oratorio *Der Siegende David (The Victorious David)* in 1717. When King Saul hears first from the female chorus and then from the combined chorus (here representing the children of Israel) about the youthful David's slaying of Goliath and his victories over the Philistines, his jealousy and fury explode as he begins the recitative, "What do I hear?"

This recitative—the text of which is, "What do I hear? Am I then sunk so low, to have this upstart boy preferr'd before me?"—is only six measures long (vocal range: C2 to D♭3) and begins with a C Major tonic triad. Ascending broken chords are used to express King Saul's increasing fits of jealousy and outrage, after which the music now modulates to f minor and descends in stages to the original starting note in the key of C Major. The musical structure of ascending broken chords or arpeggios followed by the descending chromatic scale is similar to the *Thema Regium* (King's theme) of Bach's "The Musical Offering," which was likely influenced by Handel's "Fugue in A minor," and which contains an almost identical musical structure,[62] demonstrating the importance of Handel's influence in this musical form. In addition, the change from major to minor and back again is a poignant way of showing that Saul's mental state is fragile in that his madness, represented by the minor key, changes. Indeed, there may

43

well be moments of calm after he has vented his wrath (the return to the major key), but the minor key always indicates Saul's insanity and the absence of peace and happiness.

The recitative, "To Him Ten Thousands," is then followed by the Israelite chorus singing, "David his ten thousand slew, Ten thousand praises are his due." Taunted by the chorus heaping even more praise on David, King Saul's rage bursts out again in another recitative, "To him ten thousands and to me but thousand! What can they give him more, except the kingdom?" This even shorter recitative is only four measures long (vocal range: D2 to D3). With a chord sequence of D Major, G Major, A Major, D Major, and G Major, Handel utilizes the three primary chords of tonic, subdominant, and dominant. In contrast to the previous recitative, "What do I here?," Handel utilizes here only major chords, signifying perhaps nothing more than a contrast to pave the way towards the following aria, "With Rage I Shall Burst," which starts with the second inversion of an ascending e minor broken chord, similar to the beginning of the previous recitative, "What Do I Hear?" except the key is minor rather than major.

The vocal range lies between B2 and E3, and the *tessitura*, between B3 and E3. For the string part, Handel utilizes sixteenth notes to express Saul's rage. The aria's key of e minor has the same key signature as G Major, being the latter's relative minor key. Perhaps Handel is subtly telling us here, albeit metaphorically, that just as the relative minor, characterized by the minor third interval, is a short distance harmonically from the major key, insanity is, as it were, just a short distance away from a sound mind. Indeed, Handel uses this same texture for the theme passage, "With rage I shall burst, his praises to hear!" for the accompaniment, with the orchestra playing in unison with the vocal line (Ex. 1).

Example 1. *Saul*, "With Rage I Shall Burst," mm. 1-4.

This aria is in symmetrical binary form (AB), with four measures of *ritornello* between the two sections. Even though the tempo is *Andante,* Handel keeps the drama moving apace via skillful syllabic notation, the assignment of a syllable or word to a musical note. For example, the first five quarter notes of the aria are each sung on a single-syllable word, thus moving the text forward to establish Saul's rage quickly. Then Handel moves the focus from text to music by using the more rapid sixteenth notes sung this time on a single syllable, rather than a word, in true melismatic form, as illustrated in measures 38 to 43, the musical equivalent of a vocal and angry "Grr."

Text

Charles Jennens, the librettist of both *Saul* and *Messiah*, was a very affluent writer of notable skill who had an eye for the dramatic in a story, and his libretto provides just that: David wants to be loyal to King Saul and help him, although Saul tries to take David's life; yet David shows Saul that he has the ability to kill *him*; David narrowly escapes death when Saul's javelin misses him, and the tension mounts when Saul orders his son Jonathan to kill David for him despite the brotherly love Jonathan has for David.

A long admirer of Handel's music,[63] Jennens derived the text for this dramatic story of David and Saul from 1 Samuel in the Old Testament, incidentally using the same source for Abraham Cowley's *Davideis*.[64]

The third Scene of Act 1 (Nos. 22 – 26) is from 1 Samuel, Chapter 18:6-8 (KJV).

Jennens' Libretto	The Bible (KJV)
No. 22, Chorus of Israelites Welcome, welcome, mighty king! Welcome all who conquer bring! Welcome David, warlike boy, Author of our present joy! Saul, who hast thy thousands slain, Welcome to thy friends again! David his ten thousands slew, Ten thousand praises are his due!	⁶And it came to pass as they came, when David was returned from the slaughter of the Philistine, that the women came out of all cities of Israel, singing and dancing, to meet king Saul, with tabrets, with joy, and with instruments of musick. (1 Samuel 18:6)
No. 23, *Accompagnato* Recitative What do I hear? Am I then sunk so low, To have this upstart boy preferr'd before me?	
No. 24, Chorus of Israelites David his ten thousands slew, Ten thousand praises are his due!	⁷And the women answered one another as they played, and said, Saul hath slain his thousands, and David his ten thousands. (1 Samuel 18:7)
No. 25, *Accompagnato* Recitative To him ten thousands, and to me but thousands! What can they give him more, except the kingdom?	⁸And Saul was very wroth, and the saying displeased him; and he said, They have ascribed unto David ten thousands, and to me they have ascribed but thousands: and what can he have more but the kingdom? (1 Samuel 18:8)
No. 26, The Aria With rage I shall burst his praises to hear! Oh, how I both hate the stripling, and fear! What mortal a rival in glory can bear?	

Table 1. Text of "What do I hear? … To Him Ten Thousands" and "With Rage I Shall Burst."

Verse 6 sets the scene and mood before King Saul sings his first recitative, "What Do I Hear?" The text is not in the Bible; Jennens created this dramatic moment himself to show Saul's anger and jealousy. Jennens uses verse 7 for the mixed choir, "David his ten thousands slew, Ten thousand praises are his due," that honors David's victory over the Philistines and paraphrases verse 8 for Saul's other recitative, "To Him Ten Thousands," and for the aria, "With Rage I Shall Burst." True to the text in verse 7, Handel brings in the women's chorus first, as mentioned in the previous section.

Performance Notes

In the first recitative, "What Do I Hear?," the voice line in C Major ascends as a broken chord and then descends briefly in f minor before returning to C Major again. Since King Saul is thinking about what he heard for the women's chorus rather than raging at this moment, the performer should sing this recitative with less volume (*piano*).

When singing this aria, one must prepare "the singer's body" in order to make the one-octave ascent from B2 to E3 within the space of only two measures. It is a challenging aria to sing because it is very demanding, as it requires a singer to sing with a wide vocal range as well as a relatively fast tempo. Thus, it may well require additional instruction from a trained voice teacher as this aria requires good breath support. The aria begins in the key of e minor, with Saul's rage being emphasized by all the instruments playing the same melodic line as the voice. Because of this, the performer should sing in a relatively louder voice (*forte*) in order to project over the orchestra sound with *marcato* and *sforzando* on the word "burst."

Orchestration

Both of the *accompagnato* recitatives are accompanied by selected instruments: "What Do I Hear?" by Violins I and II, Viola, Bassoon, and Organ; "To Him Ten Thousands," by Violins I and II, Viola, and Organ (Note: Bassoon is excluded in "To Him Ten Thousands"). Handel utilizes the same instruments in the recitative, "To Him Ten Thousands," and in the aria, "With Rage I Shall Burst." However, a full orchestra accompanies the choruses: Trombones I, II, and III, Carillons, Trumpets I and II, Oboes I and II, Violins I and II, Viola, and Organ.

"A Serpent, in My Bosom Warm'd" and "Has He Escap'd My Rage?"
from *Saul* by G. F. Handel

In Scene 4 of Act I, Michal, a daughter of King Saul, encourages David to play a song on his harp to soothe Saul's madness, so David accompanies himself as he sings this aria, "O Lord Whose Mercies Numberless." However, Saul's mind is still troubled, and he is bent on doing evil. David's well-meaning performance does not turn out well, as Saul goes on to sing another rage aria in Scene 5 of Act I, "A Serpent, in My Bosom Warm'd," which also serves to demonstrate Saul's mental illness. The serpent symbolizes sin as well as Satan, both of which keep the King's ears and eyes focused away from the Lord, but Saul irrationally attributes these negative qualities to David, the very person who is trying to help him. Even though David's effort to heal Saul's soul continues, Saul's rage worsens, culminating in his attempt to take David's life by throwing his javelin at him at the end of the aria, "A Serpent, in My Bosom Warm'd." However, the javelin misses its mark, and David's life is spared. Afterward, Saul commands his son, Jonathan—ironically, a beloved friend to David—to kill David on his behalf.

Saul's aria, "A Serpent, in My Bosom Warm'd," can also be classified as a "rage" song, as Smither confirms.[65] It looks like a *da capo* aria, with the A section in B♭ Major and the B section in g minor, the relative minor key of B♭ Major. However, the B section lasts only four measures, from 39 to 42, and then abruptly ends with two rapidly descending octaves of the g harmonic minor scale, as a "text painting" of King Saul's murderous intent and action, namely throwing his javelin at David (Ex. 2).

Example 2. *Saul*, "A Serpent, in My Bosom Warm'd," m.52.

The vocal range of this aria lies between B♭2 and E♭3, and the tessitura between F2 and D3. For the string part, Handel utilizes sixteenth notes to express Saul's rage as he did for the previous aria. The tempo is Allegro in *concitato* style with rapid, repeated notes as characteristic of anger and agitation, typical of the Baroque period, with similar syllabic notation as in the previous aria, including melismatic passages in measures 16 to 19 and again in measures 32 to 36.

This aria is followed by a brief dialogue-style *secco* recitative, "Has He Escap'd My Rage?" accompanied only by harpsichord continuo. This recitative is also a "rage" piece, as both the title and the ensuing lyrics suggest: "Has he escap'd my rage? I charge thee, Jonathan, upon thy duty, and all, on your allegiance, to destroy this bold aspiring youth; for while he lives, I am not safe. Reply not, but obey." It is only eight measures long (vocal range: D2 to D3) with a chord progression of the first inversion of C Major, the first inversion of A Major, d minor, the first inversion of D Major 7th, G Major, C Major, F Major, G Major, and C Major—almost all major harmonies, indicative of Saul's authority, not only as King of the realm but also as head of his family. This recitative also occurs in Scene 5 of Act I and takes approximately two-and-a-half minutes to perform.

49

Text

In Scene 5 of Act 1

Aria: A serpent, in my bosom warm'd
          Would sing me to the heart:
          But of his venom soon disarm'd,
          Himself shall feel the smart.
          Ambitious boy! now learn what danger
          It is to rouse a monarch's anger! (throws his javelin. David exit)

Secco Recitative:
          Has he escap'd my rage?
          I charge thee, Jonathan, upon thy duty,
          And all, on your allegiance, to destroy
          This bold, aspiring youth; for while he lives,
          I am not safe—Reply not, but obey.

Performance Notes

This aria begins with a ten-measure orchestral introduction, with the voice entering at the pick-up to measure 11. The first vocal line leaps from B♭2 to B♭3 with eighth notes, so the singer should prepare by establishing the "singer's body" in order to make the leaps evenly and seamlessly. It should also be noted that Handel always uses the indefinite article "a" in the phrase "a serpent" as a weak beat throughout the aria, which requires the performer to articulate the initial "s" consonant of "serpent" distinctly. Also, the "er" of "s[er]pent" should be pronounced [ɜ] instead of [ɚ] or [ɝ], to make the voice project better by lowering the tip of the tongue to touch the back of lower teeth, with the jaw relaxed. This diction issue applies equally to the words "h[ear]t," "l[ear]n," and "ang[er]."

For the melismatic movement between measures 16 and 19, and again from 32 to 36, the performer must sing well enough for all the notes to be heard distinctly, since *fioritura*, or "fast passage," typically assigns many notes to one syllable and moves quickly, demanding considerable vocal flexibility. Such melismatic passages also require a wide vocal range as well as the ability to manage a fast tempo with both small and large intervals between notes. Moreover, such passages must be sung legato, at the same time requiring performers to clarify which notes should be stressed more and which should be emphasized less. As mentioned previously, melismas call for well-trained breath control, as their performance is meant to be light and flowing, and the volume relatively low without being weak. Finally, in measures 16 through 19, every downbeat should be emphasized with the [wɔː] sound, the first part of the word "warm'd" (Ex. 3).

Example 3. *Saul*, "A Serpent, in My Bosom Warm'd," mm. 16-19.

Notice measures 17 and 18; each first 16th note is preceded by a 16th rest, so the performer should emphasize them as strong beats, as Noble's suggestion of *springboard*.[66]

Also, the repetition of descending note intervals and phrasings on the word "warm'd" in measures 16-18 occur again in measures 32-36 on the word "disarm'd." These melismatic undulations present a picture of the serpent insinuating his way into Saul to conquer his soul—highly effective text painting. Consequently, if singers master the first patterns accurately, they are already prepared for the upcoming melisma that repeats the same patterns.

Orchestration

In using Violins I and II, Viola, and Organ, Handel notably features the same instruments as in the previous aria, "With Rage I Shall Burst."

"Revenge, Timotheus Cries"

from *Alexander's Feast* by G. F. Handel

The libretto for this aria was written by Handel's friend, Newburgh Hamilton, who adapted his libretto from John Dryden's *Second Ode to St. Cecilia*, as well as from parts of his own work, *The Power of Music*. *Alexander's Feast* was premiered at the Covent Garden Theatre, London, on 19 February 1736. As mentioned in Chapter 2, during this time, Handel's most talented Italian opera singers, including castrato Senesino and bass Montagnana, left his opera company, owing to various differences of opinion, all as Handel's financial situation worsened. What was needed to attract audiences was another masterpiece, and Handel quickly obliged by composing *Alexander's Feast* in January of 1736. According to Smither, Handel did not consider it to be an oratorio. However, at that time, the genre "oratorio" was somewhat new to London audiences, but they called it an oratorio, as did the newspapers. Nowadays, we would call it a "secular oratorio," since the libretto is not taken from a sacred story or from the Bible. Even so, it was a huge success and must have encouraged Handel to consider a new direction in his musical career, by moving his creative powers away from composing Italian operas and more toward English choral works in general, and toward the oratorio in particular.

The character Timotheus in *Alexander's Feast* is a minstrel of Alexander the Great and performs several songs of praise to him at a feast held to celebrate Alexander's victory over the Persians at the city of Persepolis. This aria is the last song Timotheus sings, but the minstrel has a clear agenda, and the aria is enough to incite the already inebriated Alexander and his soldiers to set fire to the palace at Persepolis, in retaliation for a similar act committed by the Persians against the Greeks over a century before. It is a *da capo* aria, with the A section expressing Timotheus's rage and anger toward the Persians, and the B section lamenting the death of the Greeks who were killed in the above-mentioned war. The piece can thus be classified as a "rage" and "lament" aria.

Text

An aria by a bass soloist (should be sung by baritone or bass-baritone)

A section:
Revenge, revenge, Timotheus cries,
See the furies arise,
See the snakes that they rear,
How they hiss in their hair,
And the sparkles that flash from their eyes!

B section:
Behold a ghastly band,
Each a torch in his hand!
Those are Grecian ghosts, that in battle were slain,
And unbury'd, remain

Inglorious on the plain.

Performance Notes

"Revenge, Timotheus Cries" is written in typical *da capo* aria form, in which Handel was a master. Between sections A and B, there are normally differences in meter, key, and tempo. In this aria, however, Handel changes keys (from D Major to G minor) and tempos (from Allegro to Largo), but not the meter. When returning to the A section, the performer usually adds ornamentation, within this typical ABA *da capo* structure, as described in Chapter 3.

The A section is in the key of D Major, with the voice entering at measure seven after six measures of introduction by the orchestra. The aria occurs subsequent to the tenor recitative after the choir opens the second part of the oratorio. The B section, in the key of G minor, is written in a much slower tempo, about half that of the previous A section, allowing the performer the opportunity to enunciate all the consonants clearly. In the orchestral part, Handel utilizes a rhythmic pattern consisting of a dotted sixteenth note and a thirty-second note, followed by an eighth note and a thirty-second rest, and then three thirty-second notes, all to demonstrate throughout the B section Timotheus' lament and the expression of weeping at the loss of Greek lives (Ex. 4).

53

Example 4. *Alexander's Feast*, "Revenge, Timotheus Cries," B section rhythms.

Although the meter remains constant, the tempo does not. To express Timotheus' rage, Handel employs a faster tempo in the A section but a slower one in the B section, where the emphasis is on lament. The vocal range lies between G2 and E4, and the *tessitura* is between E3 and D4. This aria takes approximately eight minutes to perform.

Despite anecdotes claiming that Handel struggled with the English language, Lang assures us that this was not the case. Citing Handel's contemporary, historian Sir John Hawkins, who spoke from personal knowledge, Lang asserts:

> The historian [Hawkins] acknowledges that Handel "pronounced the English as the Germans do," but his estimate of Handel's proficiency in English differs markedly from that implied in anecdotes. "Of the English also he had such a degree of knowledge, as to be susceptible of the beauties of our best poets; so that in the multiplicity of his compositions to English words, he seldom stood in the need of assistance."[67]

This aria also confirms Handel's knowledge at least of English grammar if not pronunciation, and he certainly knew where proper word stress should occur. For instance, he places the second syllable "-venge" of "revenge" on the first downbeat, a strong beat, which occurs consistently throughout the A section. In addition, Handel is familiar with vocal technique and deals with the *fioritura* passages naturally. For example, in measures 17 and 18, he utilizes the word painting technique as the second inversion of the A Major broken chord ascends with the text "See the Furies arise" (Ex. 5).

Example 5. *Alexander's Feast*, "Revenge, Timotheus Cries," mm. 17-18.

Handel also knows how this dramatic moment should be established, as he begins the pick-up to the soloist's entry by having the accompaniment start an A Major chord ascent first, introducing the build-up to Timotheus' rage naturally, then having both the soloist and orchestra continue the ascent together in a dynamic crescendo.

These compositional skills demonstrate Handel's ability to manage both melody and word stress in the English language and indicate why he is often called a supreme melodist and why his arias have been favored by singers for so long.

An example of a melismatic section with the prime notes marked is shown in Example 6. Between mm. 12 and 15, for example, the word "cries," which begins the melismatic movement, should be sung with the [ɑ] vowel. This also applies to the mid vowel "a" of the word "sparkles" in mm. 24-25 and 37-40. Every strong beat is emphasized as well. Furthermore, the performer should emphasize every downbeat. There are two D4s and two B3s that should be emphasized in measure 14 equally (indicated with circles). The performer should take a breath between the two notes as well.

Example 6. *Alexander's Feast*, "Revenge, Timotheus Cries," mm. 12-15.

In measure 41, however, the word "flash" should be sung with an open [a] to reflect the phonetically higher vowel of the word. The technical demands of the *fioritura* are the same as those mentioned in the previous aria, namely well-controlled breath, with a delivery that is equally light and flowing, and with the same volume as before: relatively low without being weak.

The aria should be performed by either a baritone or a bass-baritone, and for the final note, G2, of the B section (m. 24), the word "plain" should be sung with the vowel [ɛ], instead of [eɪ] (Ex. 7), so that the low pitch can be articulated. Just as a singer modifies certain vowels while singing above the *passaggio*—the transition area between vocal registers—in order to maintain a smooth tone and even timbre between the registers, so the baritone or bass-baritone singer should do the same when singing lower than A♭2.

Example 7. *Alexander's Feast*, "Revenge, Timotheus Cries," m. 24.

on   the   plain.

Orchestration

Handel utilizes Oboe I and II, Basson (Fagotti) I and II, Horn (Corno) I and II, Trumpet (Tromba) I and II, Timpani, Violino I and II, Viola, Bassi, and Continuo in general. For this aria, Handel utilizes Trumpets, Oboes, Violins, Viola, Double Bass (Bassi), and Continuo for the A section, but simply excludes the trumpets for the B section.

℃

"Thus Saith the Lord" and "But Who May Abide the Day of His Coming?"
from *Messiah* by G. F. Handel

As the best-known work in the genre of oratorio, Handel's *Messiah* has been performed somewhere every year since Handel composed it in 1741,[68] and is still considered a favorite around the world, especially at Christmas time. Handel composed his masterpiece in just 24 days in the late summer of 1741, and it premiered in Dublin in 1742, and again a year later in 1743 in London. The libretto is a scriptural text compiled by Charles Jennens from the King James Bible, including verses from both the Old Testament (the Prophets and Psalms) and the New Testament (the Gospels, Epistles of Paul, and Revelation), depicting the prophecies about, and the advent of, the Savior of the world.

"Thus Saith the Lord" is in the form of an *accompagnato* recitative, and sounds urgent and foreboding, seeming on the surface to reflect only God's rage. However,

Handel intended it to describe not only God's divine anger towards His disobedient children but also His majesty and His power, which pervade the whole of Part I, which centers on the Nativity, or the birth of Christ.

The aria "But Who May Abide the Day of His Coming?" also contains typical rage elements, in which Handel uses melismatic passages on the phrase "a refiner's fire" as text painting and as a reminder that, although the Lord's power and majesty are often meant to *refine* rather than destroy, to save rather than condemn—if His children so choose—the process is still often a dramatic and harrowing one. Even so, this saving aspect of the Lord's majesty and power is established right from the beginning of *Messiah* in "Comfort Ye My People," the opening tenor recitative.

Both "Thus Saith the Lord " and "But Who May Abide the Day of His Coming?" describe the first and second coming of the Lord and bring good news and expected peace to those who trust in Him, but for those who refuse Him as their Lord and Savior, there will be a day of judgment, a day of God's wrath and punishment.

Text

The text of "Thus Saith the Lord" is taken from Haggai 2:6-7 and Malachi 3:1. The text of the aria "But Who May Abide the Day of His Coming?" is from Malachi 3:2. However, the librettist, Jennens, clearly did not utilize every word of the Biblical text, as Table 2 shows:

Jennens's Libretto	**The Bible (KJV)**
The Arioso	
Thus saith the Lord of hosts: Yet once a little while, and I will shake the heav'ns and the earth, the sea, and the dry land, and I will shake all nations, and the desire of all nations shall come.	[6]For thus saith the Lord of hosts; Yet once, it is a little while, and I will shake the heavens, and the earth, and the sea, and the dry land; [7]And I will shake all nations, and the desire of all nations shall come: and I will fill this house with glory, saith the Lord of hosts. (Haggai 2:6-7)

The *Accompagnato* Recitative

The Lord, whom ye seek, shall suddenly come to his temple, ev'n the messenger of the covenant, whom ye delight in; behold he shall come, saith the Lord of hosts.	[1]Behold I will send my messenger, and he shall prepare the way before me: and the Lord, whom ye seek, shall suddenly come to his temple, even the messenger of the covenant, whom ye delight in: behold, he shall come, saith the Lord of hosts. (Malachi 3:1)

The Aria

But who may abide the day of his coming? And who shall stand when he appeareth? For he is like a refiner's fire.	[2]But who may abide the day of his coming? and who shall stand when he appeareth? for he is like a refiner's fire, and like fullers' soap. (Malachi 3:2)

Table 2. Text of "Thus Saith the Lord" and
"But Who May Abide the Day of His Coming?"

Performance Notes

This aria "But Who May Abide" takes approximately six minutes to perform. As mentioned previously, "Thus Saith the Lord" is usually designated as an *accompagnato* recitative for a bass soloist. However, more accurately, owing to the melismatic movements through measure 22 (from Haggai 2:6-7), it is an *arioso*, a form that lies somewhere between a pure recitative and a full aria. This section is followed by a genuine *accompagnato* recitative (from Malachi 3:1) between mm. 23 and 30. Consequently, it can be more accurately designated as an *arioso* followed by an accompanied recitative.

Handel's original intention was for a bass soloist to sing both pieces—"Thus Saith the Lord" and "But Who May Abide the Day of His Coming?"—in the key of D minor, and at the Dublin premiere in 1742 both were, in fact, sung by a bass soloist in that key, with no *prestissimo* sections. However, for the performance in 1749 in London, Handel wrote a new version of the aria, "But Who May Abide the Day of His Coming?" for countertenor. The change seems to have lasted, for "Thus Saith the Lord' is now always sung by a bass soloist, and the aria, "But Who May Abide the Day of His Coming?" performed by either a bass, a female alto/mezzo, or a countertenor. There is also a soprano version in the key of A minor, so who performs the set and in which key depends both on the conductor's preference and on the soloist's ability and range.

The accompaniment begins simply with ascending chords in D minor. Then the voice enters boldly on a descending melodic line in measure 2 starting with D4; therefore, the singer should prepare the "singer's body," as explained at the beginning of this chapter, to be able to sing the phrases energetically so as to express God's majesty, especially in the opening phrase, "Thus saith the Lord, the Lord of Hosts" (Ex. 8).

Example 8. *Messiah*, "Thus, Saith the Lord," mm. 1-3.

When the performer sings the first consonant of "Thus," as it is the voiced linguadental fricative continuant [ð], it should be articulated right before the downbeat and then the vowel [ʌ] should on the downbeat. Once the performer begins this part with a correct resonance it is much easier to maintain it. As Miller remarks, this consonant is a way of balancing the resonance, "The accompanying 'buzzy' feeling that results from sustaining the consonant [ð] is generally strongly felt in the upper jaw and *masque* areas."[69]

Handel uses the melismas as text painting on the words "shake" and "desire." For the word "shake," as the melisma moves, the singer should sing an open and taller [ɛ] vowel in order to make seamless transitions by maintaining the same placement. For the first vowel of the word "desire," the performer should sing an [ɪ] vowel, and for the second vowel, the performer should sing an [ɑ] vowel, with the completion of the diphthong at the end of the word. A singer must articulate the final consonant of every melismatic movement accurately, the "k" consonant of the word "shake," for example, since the word on which the melisma is based cannot be identified on the basis of the melisma vowel alone; the final consonant is needed for the word to be accurately identified and understood. As usual, each strong beat of the melisma should be emphasized. The vocal range is between B♭2 to D4, with the *tessitura* ranging from F3 to D4.

The "refiner's fire" metaphor reflects both the positive and the negative aspects of Malachi's message. The literal refining of metal produces a purer metal, so the refining is a positive process, as indeed it is for those who accept the Lord's refining via willing repentance. However, for those who reject refinement, the Lord's offer of purification is seen as negative and unwanted. These people will certainly not be able to stand "when He appeareth." This duality can be reflected in the performance by singing one repetition of the phrase "like a refiner's fire" *legato* to reflect the Lord's grace and one repetition more staccato (*agitato*) to reflect the consequences of willfully rejecting it.

The aria "But Who May Abide the Day of His Coming?" is also in the key of D minor. For the meter, Handel uses 3/8 for the "larghetto" part and 4/4 for the "prestissimo" section; therefore, the order of meters for this aria is 3/8, 4/4, 3/8, and 4/4. Thus, the form of this aria is AA, BA, B with alternating tempos and meters—a type of ritornello structure that was common in the Baroque.

The vocal range is between G2 and E♭4, with the *tessitura* between F3 and D4. In the "adagio" section in measures 148 to 159, a singer would normally add more notes to create a dramatic ending, i.e., as a cadenza, an example of which appears in the same measures in the 1992 version by Watkins Shaw. However, it is left to the individual performer to decide which notes to add.

There are ample resources regarding how to perform *Messiah* arias. In their book, *Face to Face with Orchestra and Chorus*, Moses, Demaree, and Olmes provide useful information, such as tempo suggestions, for performing *Messiah* arias. There are even discussions of whether to feel the beginning tempo of "But Who May Abide" in one or in three (meter: 3/8). The authors even discuss bowing techniques that influence the overall style. Looking at these arias through the conductor's lens also helps the performer prepare to sing arias with an orchestra. From Shrock's *Handel's Messiah: A Performance Practice Handbook*, the performer can gain general knowledge about performance practice of the Baroque era and then specific information on the recitatives and arias. Shrock includes ideas on tempo, articulation, phrasing, and ideas for ornamentation in each aria. He notes the slightly different articulations for "Thus Saith the Lord, the Lord of Hosts" on pages 34-35. He includes his suggested ornamentations above the original melodies so that the performer can see them alongside one another for comparison. From the Van Camp text, *A Practical Guide for Performing, Teaching, and Singing Messiah*, the performer can obtain hints and performance notes as well as interpretative guidelines for each aria in *Messiah*. Thus, these books can be additional resources for those who want to learn how to sing arias from *Messiah*.

Orchestration

Throughout *Messiah* Handel's orchestration generally consists of two Oboes, strings (2 Violins and Viola) and Basso Continuo provided by Bassoon, Harpsichord, Cello, and Violone (Contrabass). In addition, Handel uses 2 Trumpets and Timpani for several movements, such as in Scene 4 of Part I of the choral movement "Glory to God in the Highest"; in Scene 7 of Part II, the last "Hallelujah" chorus; and in Scene 2 of Part III, the bass aria "The Trumpet Shall Sound."

For these selections, Handel employs strings (Violins, Violas, and Basses) with Continuo.

ര

"Why Do the Nations so Furiously Rage Together?"

from *Messiah* by G. F. Handel

This is another typical rage aria written in the key of C Major, with the text of Jennens's libretto taken from King David's messianic psalm in Psalms 2: 1, 2. It takes from two to five minutes to perform, depending on the cuts as well as the tempo. The full version is in the *da-capo* form; however, there is also a dramatically shortened, non *da-capo* version, which Handel wrote for the Dublin premiere. In this version, the B section is followed, not by a return to the first section, but by the chorus "Let Us Break Their Bonds Asunder." The aria appears in Scene 6 of Part II of *Messiah*, which centers on the crucifixion, resurrection, and ascension of the Savior.

Text

As mentioned above, the text is based on Psalms 2:1-2 (Table 3), and the second section, the B section of the aria, is followed not by a return to the first section but by the chorus "Let Us Break Their Bonds Asunder," which is also from Psalm Chapter 2, but verse 3. Although the two texts are clearly related, the music, however, is not. According to Smither, The chorus "Let Us Break Their Bonds Asunder" is a logical continuation and completion of the aria "Why Do the Nations so Furiously Rage Together," although the two are not melodically related."[70]

Jennens's Libretto	The Bible (KJV)
The Aria	
Why do the nations so furiously rage together, and why do the people imagine a vain thing? The kings of the earth rise up, and the rulers take counsel together against the Lord and against his Anointed.	Psalm 2:1 – Why do the heathen rage, and the people imagine a vain thing? Psalm 2:2 – The kings of the earth set themselves, and the rulers take counselor together, against the LORD, and against his anointed, saying

Table 3. Text of "Why Do the Nations so Furiously Rage Together?"

Performance Notes

This aria contains the most difficult and challenging melismatic sections of the 11 arias chosen for this study. These melismatic passages move in triplets based on the words "rage," "imagine," "counsel," and "anointed." The triplets themselves follow a predictable pattern. When the note interval in the first triplet is a half step (A of Ex. 9), the interval of the last two notes of the following triplet is a major third down; however, if the note interval in the first triplet is a whole step (B of Ex. 9), the interval of the last two notes of the next triplet is a minor third down, throughout the melisma. In other words, a half step down from the last two notes of a triplet is followed by a major third down in the last two notes of the following triplet, and a whole step down from the last two notes of a triplet is followed by a minor third down in the last two notes of the following triplet (Ex. 9).

Example 9. *Messiah*, "Why Do the Nations so Furiously Rage
Together?" mm. 23-24.

In melismatic passages, every first note of a triplet should be stressed as discussed for previous arias, and every final consonant—usually occurring at or toward the end of every melisma—should be strongly articulated for the word to be accurately identified as either "rage," "imagine," "counsel," or "anointed." In addition to that, Miller recommends practicing the first note of the triplet group, and then, adding the rest of the notes with slower tempo until learning all the pitches thoroughly of the melismas.[71]

There are fourteen measures of orchestral introduction before the bass soloist enters at measure fifteen with an ascending C Major arpeggio, followed by the descending scale in Handel's traditional idiom in his "rage" arias (Ex. 10). Indeed, we find a similar pattern in the aria "With Rage I Shall Burst" from *Saul*, as mentioned earlier.

Example 10. *Messiah*, "Why Do the Nations so Furiously Rage Together?"
mm. 15-18.

In addition, Shrock also provides his ideas of ornamentation for this aria on pages 87 and 89 of his *Handel's Messiah: A Performance Practice Handbook* so that the performer can see them alongside one another for comparison.

Orchestration

For this aria, Handel employs the same instruments as for "Thus Saith the Lord," strings (Violins, Violas, and Basses) and Continuo.

"The Walls Are Levell'd" and "See, the Raging Flames Arise"

from *Joshua* by G. F. Handel

The oratorio *Joshua* premiered in 1748 at the Covent Garden Theatre in London, although Handel had finished composing *Joshua* one year earlier, in 1747. The libretto of *Joshua* was written by Thomas Morell, one of Handel's chief collaborators, who also provided texts for Handel's *Judas Maccabaeus*, *Theodora*, *Jephtha*, and more. The oratorio *Joshua* is based on the Biblical story of Joshua from the Old Testament, though Morell added stories of his own, such as the love interest between Othniel and Achsah.

Through Moses' leadership, and the ensuing miracle of the parting of the Red Sea, God saves the Children of Israel, the descendants of Abraham, from enslavement in Egypt, but Moses does not get to see the Promised Land himself. That assignment and privilege is given to Joshua, the son of Nun, who leads the Israelites into the Promised Land of Canaan after Moses is taken out of their midst. In this recitative, Joshua's military commander, Jephunneh's son, Caleb, who was sent by Joshua into Canaan to spy out the land, describes in Scene 1 of Act II in his *secco* recitative, "The Walls Are Levell'd," the dramatic collapse of Jericho, as the title suggests. With text from Chapter 6 of the Old Testment book of Joshua, Caleb sings the aria "See, the Raging Flames Arise."

Text
Secco Recitative, Caleb:

The walls are levell'd, pour the chosen bands,
With hostile gore imbrue your thirsty hands,
Set palaces and temples in a blaze,
Sap the foundations, and the bulwarks raze.
But oh, remember, in the bloody strife,
To spare the hospitable Rahab's life.

Aria, Caleb:

See, the raging flames arise,
Hear, the dismal groans and cries!
The fatal day of wrath is come,
Proud Jericho hath met her doom.

Performance Notes

This aria is a typical rage aria, written in *bravura aria* style, which requires a high level of performance skill. The aria is about God's wrath upon Jericho after God promises He will deliver the city into the hands of Israel, as recorded in Joshua, Chapter 6 verse 2. The aria takes approximately three minutes thirty seconds to perform and demands a sophisticated vocal technique.

The vocal range of the recitative is between E3 and C4, and for the aria between A2 and E4. The chord progression of the recitative in the key of A minor is the first inversion of E Major, A minor, the first inversion of C Major, the first inversion of f# diminished, the first inversion of G Major, the first inversion of B Major, the first inversion of E minor, the first inversion of f# diminished seventh, and the half cadence (ii7 (V/V) and V). There are two moods that the singer should distinguish here by using a different tone quality or color for each of them. These moods are divided in the libretto by the word "but." The first part, "The walls are levell'd, pour the chosen bands, With hostile gore imbrue your thirsty hands, Set palaces and temples in a blaze, Sap the foundations, and the bulwarks raze," emphasizes God's fury, and the second part, "But oh, remember, in the bloody strife, To spare the hospitable Rahab's life" expresses God's grace and love, inviting a softer and warmer tone.

The aria is in A minor and contains typical features of Handel's rage arias in general, such as a relatively faster tempo, *Allegro,* in this case, *concitato* movements with many repeated sixteenth notes and melismatic phrasings. It also contains rising scales as text-painting to manifest the intensity of God's fury. Handel uses this text painting to emphasize the words, "arise," "wrath," and "flames." For example, measures 17-19 contain almost identical melismatic phrasing, with the exception of the last two notes, to measures 57-59, all on the main vowel of the word "flames" (Ex. 11).

Example 11. *Joshua*, "See, the Raging Flames Arise," mm. 17-19 and 57-59.

If the performer learns the note pattern in measures 17-18 accurately, with the stress on the prime notes, i.e., on every downbeat, then the repeated sequence in measures 57-59 should present no additional challenges. Furthermore, in measure 58, the performer should take a breath between C4 and B3 (between the 8th and 16th notes), which is on the third beat. This is in order to sing D4 and E4 well later in measure 59. When the performer learns the last measure (m. 19) thoroughly, then adding the preceding measures, until mastering the whole section of melismas, helps to build up the breath management as well.

Orchestration

For this aria, Handel scores strings (Violins, Violas, Cellos, and Double-Basses) with Continuo which he also utilizes for the *secco* recitative.

5

Mendelssohn's Oratorio Arias from a Performer's Perspective

"Vertilge sie, Herr Zebaoth"

from *Paulus* by F. Mendelssohn

Given the conversion of Mendelssohn and his family from Judaism to Christianity (see Chapter 2), Mendelssohn's choice of the story of St. Paul's conversion for his first oratorio is understandable. In fact, both of Mendelssohn's oratorios, *Paulus* and *Elijah*, were relevant to his Jewish heritage, not only because the apostle Paul, like Mendelssohn himself, was a Jewish convert, but also because Mendelssohn saw Christianity as the "universalization of Judaism."[72]

In 1835, while Mendelssohn was composing his first oratorio, his revered father, Abraham, whose opinion Mendelssohn always sought regarding a new composition, died. This tragic event was a trigger for Mendelssohn to finish *Paulus* as a tribute to his father. The oratorio premiered in May 1836, in German at the Lower Rhine Music Festival in Düsseldorf, and the English premiere took place in Liverpool in the same year, in a version translated by Karl Klingemann. In the following year of 1837, Mendelssohn conducted the oratorio at the Birmingham Festival, where about ten years later his second oratorio, *Elijah*, also premiered. The U. S. premiere took place in Boston, also in 1837.

Mendelssohn intended his first oratorio to be a sermon, a musical tool for edifying congregations, just as Handel and Bach had hoped for in their own music.

Text

According to Smither, Mendelssohn began writing the storyline of *Paulus* in 1832, and completed it later with the help of two friends, Adolf Bernhard Marx and Julius Schubring, who assisted him in selecting proper Bible verses.[73] Schubring, a pastor and theologian, as well as a childhood friend of Mendelssohn, is credited with the libretto because Mendelssohn favored his version over Marx's.[74] The Bible-based libretto, from both the Old and New Testaments, is based mainly on the Acts of the Apostles. This rage aria, "Vertilge sie, Herr Zebaoth," is taken from Psalm 59:13; 83:18; and 69:24. The German translation is from the German Luther Bible, whereas the English translation is from the King James Version (Table 4).

	Libretto	The Bible (GLB and KJV)
	The Aria	
German	Vertilge sie, Herr Zebaoth, wie Stoppeln vor dem Ferer! Sie wollen nicht erkennen, daß du mit deinem Namen heißest Herr allein, der Höchste in aller Welt. Laß deinen Zorn sie treffen, verstummen müssen sie!	[13]Vertilge sie ohne alle Gnade; vertilge sie, daß sie nichts seien und innewerden, daß Gott Herrscher sei in Jakob, in aller Welt. (Sela.) (Psalm 59:13)
		[18]so werden sie erkennen, daß du mit deinem Namen heißest HERR allein und der Höchste in aller Welt. (Psalm 83:18)
		[24]Gieße deine Ungnade auf sie, und dein grimmiger Zorn ergreife sie. (Psalm 69:24)

English	Consume them all, Lord Sabaoth, consume all these Thine enemies. Behold, they will not know Thee, that Thou, our Great Jehovah, art the Lord alone, the Highest over all the world. Pour out Thine indignation, and let them feel Thy power.	¹³Consume them in wrath, consume them, that they may not be: and let them know that God ruleth in Jacob unto the ends of the earth. Selah. (Psalm 59:13)
		¹⁸That men may know that thou, whose name alone is JEHOVAH, art the most high over all the earth. (Psalm 83:18)
		²⁴Pour out thine indignation upon them, and let thy wrathful anger take hold of them. (Psalm 69:24)

Table 4. Text of "Vertilge sie, Herr Zebaoth"

Performance Notes

"Vertilge sie, Herr Zebaoth" is a typical rage aria, but without melismas, sung by Saul in Part I, No. 12, followed by the tenor recitative "Saulus aber zerstörte die Gemeinde" ("Now Saul made havoc of the Church"). This is prior to Saul's conversion. Right before Saul sings this rage aria, the Jews stone Stephen, accusing him of blasphemy, as Saul looks on with approval. Mendelssohn most likely considered Saul's persecution of Christians to be similar to what he and his family were going through at this time in Germany. Thus, the performer should be able to demonstrate Saul's voice as persecutor, with a relatively louder and forceful tone, by using *tenuto* and *sforzando* for the emphasized notes. After this aria, Saul's conversion takes place, as the female choir, representing the Lord's voice from heaven, sings, "Saul! was verfolgst du mich?" (*Saul, Saul, why persecutest thou Me?*). Jesus appears to Saul and gives him instructions. Saul's conversion comes at a cost, for he is blinded by the glory of the light and, ironically, is converted from being a persecutor to one who will himself soon be persecuted as an apostle of the Lord. Mendelssohn's use of a women's chorus here is evidence of Handel's influence in this choral form, since Handel utilizes the female choir to praise David's victories in *Saul*, prior to the recitative, "What Do I Hear?"

The aria takes approximately three minutes to perform. The vocal range lies between B2 and D4, and *tessitura* between F3 and D4. The tempo mark is *Allegro molto*, and the key of the aria is B minor. The form of the aria is through-composed, so it displays well what the composer wanted to say. The melodic line manifests the state of rage of Saul by leaps (both up and down) and by a relatively faster tempo. In the four-measure introduction, the brass parts and timpani's four-note motif is established and appears throughout the aria (Ex. 12). Interestingly the first four-measure introduction is almost identical to the ending of the aria from mm. 109-12.

Example 12. *Paulus*, "Vertilge sie, Herr Zebaoth," mm. 1-4.

Since the original language of this aria is German, the performer must be able to articulate all the consonants precisely, including consonant clusters, such as "Stoppeln," "erkennen," and "Höchste," as well as final consonants, bearing in mind that in German these are all unvoiced.

Orchestration

The full orchestra consists of strings: Violins, Violas, Cellos, and Contrabasses; woodwind instruments: Flutes, Oboes, Clarinets, and Bassoons; brass: Horns, Trumpets, Trombones, Serpent (modern tuba); Organ, and Timpani.

For the aria "Vertilge sie, Herr Zebaoth," Mendelssohn utilizes Oboe, Bassoon, Trumpet, Timpani, and Strings.

಄

"Gott, sei mir gnädig"

from *Paulus* by F. Mendelssohn

This prayer-like aria, "Gott, sei mir gnädig," appears in Part I, No. 18, right after Saul's conversion. When Ananias lays hands on Saul's eyes, his sight is restored, and he is fully healed from being blind. At that moment, Paul decides to begin his journey of ministry to proclaim and spread the Word of God to the Gentiles. In Section A Paul prays for forgiveness for what he previously did wrong in the eyes of the Lord. Then in Section B he asks for the Lord's help on his journey. Now Paul becomes a disciple of Jesus Christ and submits himself to his divine calling.

Text:

The text is based on the book of Psalm 51:1, 11, and 17 for A section and verses 13 and 15 for B section (Table 5).

	Libretto	The Bible (GLB and KJV)
		The Aria
German	**A** Sektion:	
	Gott, sei mir gnädig nach deiner Güte, und tilge meine Sünden nach deiner großen Barmherzigkeit. Verwirf mich nicht von deinem Angesicht, und nimm deinen heiligen Geist night von mir. Ein geängstetes und zerschlagenes Herz wirst du, Gott, nicht verachten.	¹Gott, sei mir gnädig nach deiner Güte und tilge meine Sünden nach deiner großen Barmherzigkeit. (Psalm 51:1) ¹¹Verwirf mich nicht von deinem Angesicht und nimm deinen heiligen Geist nicht von mir. (Psalm 51:11) ¹⁷Die Opfer, die Gott gefallen, sind ein geängsteter Geist; ein geängstetes und zerschlagenes Herz wirst du, Gott, nicht verachten. (Psalm 51:17)
	B Sektion:	
	Denn ich will die Übertreter deine Wege lehren, daß sich die Sünder zu dir bekehren. Herr, tue meine Lippen auf, daß mein Mund deinen Ruhm verkündige. Und tilge meine Sünden nach deiner großen Barm herzigkeit. Herr, verwirf mich nicht!	¹³Ich will die Übertreter deine Wege lehren, daß sich die Sünder zu dir bekehren. (Psalm 51:13) ¹⁵Herr, tue meine Lippen auf, daß mein Mund deinen Ruhm verkündige. (Psalm 51:15)

It Is Enough!

English | **A** section:

A section (left)	Scripture (right)
God, have mercy upon me, and blot out my transgressions according to Thy loving kindness, yea, even for Thy mercy's sake. Deny me not, cast me not away from Thy presence, and take not Thy Spirit from me, Lord. Lord, a broken and a contrite heart is offered before Thee.	¹Have mercy upon me, O God, according to thy lovingkindness: according unto the multitude of thy tender mercies blot out my transgressions. (Psalm 51:1) ¹¹Cast me not away from thy presence; and take not thy holy spirit from me. (Psalm 51:11) ¹⁷The sacrifices of God are a broken spirit: a broken and a contrite heart, O God, thou wilt not despise. (Psalm 51:17)
B section: I will speak of Thy salvation, I will teach transgressors, and all the sinners shall be converted unto Thee. Then open Thou my lips, Lord, and my mouth shall show forth Thy glorious praise.	¹³Then will I teach transgressors thy ways; and sinners shall be converted unto thee. (Psalm 51:13) ¹⁵O Lord, open thou my lips; and my mouth shall shew forth thy praise. (Psalm 51:15)

Table 5. Text of "Gott, sei mir gnädig"

Performance Notes

This aria takes approximately four minutes and thirty seconds to perform. The A section (a prayer for forgiveness) is a relatively slower tempo than the B section (a prayer about Paul's mission). The tempo markings are *Adagio* (A), *Allegro maestoso* (B), and *Adagio* (A') and the tonal structure is B minor (A), G and then D Major (B), and B Major (A'). The vocal line begins on the second beat of the fifth measure after a four-measure introduction. The is a typical *da-capo* aria, ABA'. Section A is a lyrical section in which Saul repents of his sins before the Lord, and Section B is dramatic in displaying his dedication to serving the Lord. Thus the performer should be able to express Saul's different emotional states between these two sections by using different timbres. In the A section, for example, where the repentant Saul shows a deep longing for God's mercy and an eagerness to be forgiven, a warm and rich tone color conveys this; for the B section, where Saul commits to serving the Lord, an energized and more cheerful tone color is appropriate. Between the A and B sections, Mendelssohn repeats the four-measure introduction as an interlude, and suddenly the key changes to G Major from B minor to signal Paul's change in mood, namely from regretful (minor) to cheerful (major). Mendelssohn adds brass instruments to the B section to emphasize this. The vocal range (B2-D4) and the *tessitura* (F3-D4) are exactly the same as in the previous aria, "Vertilge sie, Herr Zebaoth."

Orchestration
Mendelssohn utilizes Oboes, a Bassoon, and Strings for the A and A' sections, and Trumpets, Trombones, and Strings for the B section.

03

"Draw Near, All Ye People, Come to Me!" and "Lord God of Abraham"
from *Elijah* by F. Mendelssohn

Mendelssohn's second oratorio, *Elijah*, was premiered on August 26th in 1846, at the Birmingham Festival in Birmingham's Town Hall, where Mendelssohn's first oratorio, *Paulus*, was performed under his baton. It was based on the story and events in the life of the Biblical prophet Elijah, from the books of First and Second Kings. Mendelssohn's earliest-known mention of *Elijah* dates from August 1836, about three months after the premiere of *Paulus* and about ten years prior to the new oratorio.[75] As mentioned in Chapter 3, Mendelssohn displayed keen interest in Handel's oratorios and, as he was preparing to publish them in a new edition, included them in his regular concert repertoire between 1836 and 1846. Consequently, Mendelssohn had every opportunity to be influenced by Handel's oratorios as he worked on *Elijah*, and influenced he certainly was. For example, Mendelssohn's "Is not His Word Like a Fire" from *Elijah* sounds very similar to the B section of "For He Is Like a Refiner's Fire" from Handel's "But Who May Abide the Day of His Coming?" from *Messiah*.

Text

According to Smither, Mendelssohn really wanted to have the libretto of *Elijah* prepared by his boyhood friend Karl Klingemann, who had already translated *Paulus* from the German into English and who was already in London serving as secretary to the Hanoverian Legation. However, Klingemann never got it done, despite Mendelssohn's urgings for him to finish it.[76] Therefore, Mendelssohn decided to complete it with Schubring, the librettist of *Paulus*. The English translations were by William Bartholomew for the Birmingham premiere.

Schubring's Libretto	The Bible (KJV)
The Recitative	
Draw near, all ye people: come to me!	[30]"And Elijah said unto all the people, Come near unto me. And all the people came near unto him. And he repaired the altar of the LORD that was broken down." (1 Kings 18:30)
The Aria	
Lord God of Abraham, Isaac and Israel, this day let it be known that Thou art God and that I am Thy servant. Lord God of Abraham, oh show to all this people that I have done these things according to Thy word. Oh hear me, Lord, and answer me. Lord God of Abraham, Isaac and Israel, oh hear me and answer me, and show this people that Thou art Lord God and let their hearts again be turned.	[36]And it came to pass at the time of the offering of the evening sacrifice, that Elijah the prophet came near, and said, LORD God of Abraham, Isaac, and of Israel, let it be known this day that thou art God in Israel, and that I am thy servant, and that I have done all these things at thy word. [37]Hear me, O LORD, hear me, that this people may know that thou art the LORD God, and that thou hast turned their heart back again. (1 Kings 18:36 - 37)

Table 6. Text of "Draw near, all ye people ... Lord God of Abraham"

Performance Notes

In this part of the oratorio, Elijah proposes a contest between himself (with the help of the Lord) and four hundred and fifty prophets of Baal to determine whose god is the real God in Israel in the hopes that the people with turn back to Him. Elijah summons the people and the prophets of Baal and Asherah[77] to Mount Carmel. Elijah asks his people, "How long halt ye between two opinions? if the LORD be God, follow him: but if Baal, then follow him. And the people answered him not a word." Elijah presents to the people his plan, whereby the two parties, Elijah and the prophets of Baal, would each build an altar and prepare a bullock for the evening sacrifice. The god that sent down fire to consume the sacrifice would be declared the true God. The people agree, answering, "It is well spoken" (1 Kings 18:24).

The prophets of Baal call upon their god the whole day, but there is no answer even though they show their dedication to Baal by cutting themselves with knives. This is the scenario prior to Elijah's aria, "Lord God of Abraham," between Nos. 11 and 13 and based on 1 Kings Chapter 18, verses 26-29. The chorus practically shouts to Baal to beg him to hear and answer the prayers of his prophets, by repeating at the end of No. 13 four times the phrase "gib uns Antwort!" without any orchestral accompaniment. This dramatic moment occurs right before Elijah sings his beautiful and peaceful prayer "Lord God of Abraham." Mendelssohn excludes all the brass instruments, except horns, and timpani, although he utilizes brass instruments for the previous movement for the chorus. The tempo also changes from *Allegro molto* for the chorus (No. 13) to *Adagio* for Elijah's aria (No. 14). By means of these changes in text, tempo, and dynamics, Mendelssohn is conveying to us that the Lord is in control and that He is more likely to be reached, not by tumultuous noise and shouting, as demonstrated by the prophets of Baal, but by the "still small voice." The singer's performance should reflect this.

The recitative "Draw Near, All Ye People, Come to Me" and the aria "Lord God of Abraham" take approximately three minutes and fifty seconds to perform. This prayer-like aria is sung by Elijah (baritone), in Scene 3 of Part I, No 14. The recitative is a transition from F# minor to Eb Major, which is the key of the aria, the vocal range being from Bb2 to Eb4, and *tessitura* between F3 and D4. The aria begins with the word "Lord" on the highest pitch of the song, namely Eb4, so the performer should prepare the "singer's body" to sing the Eb4 effortlessly and smoothly by placing the back "o" vowel of "Lord" more forward, like the [ɑ] vowel of "God" (Ex. 13).

75

Example 13. *Elijah*, "Lord God of Abraham," m. 7.

Lord God of A - bra - ham,

Elijah's recitative "Draw Near, All Ye People, Come to Me" serves not only to gather the people of Israel on Mount Carmel but also to instruct them to repair "the altar of the Lord" demolished by Jezebel (1 Kings 18:30-35). The six-measure introduction to the aria signifies the passing of time required to accomplish this. In the meantime, the prophets of Baal fail to bring down fire despite their day-long petition. Now it is time for Elijah, via his prayer, to call upon the Lord to reveal who the true God is by sending down fire, as a sign to both the apostate prophets of Baal and to the people of Israel, who desperately need to return to their God (1 Kings 18:36-38). Interestingly, the Viola (rather than the Violin) along with Flute and B♭ Clarinet, play the melodic line in the introduction, a quiet representation of Elijah's unshaken faith as a servant of the Lord. Therefore, the performer should be able to represent Elijah's faith in the Lord by using a quality of vocal tone that expresses warmth, buoyancy, and hope.

The Lord answers Elijah's prayer immediately by sending down fire that consumes everything on and around the altar: the wood, the dust, the stones, the water, and the burnt sacrifice. By this, the Lord manifests Himself as a faithful God, as the people fall on their faces and acknowledge the true God of Israel (1 Kings 18:39).

Orchestration

For this oratorio, Mendelssohn's instrumentation is for Woodwind: Flutes, Oboes, Clarinets, Bassoons; Brass: Trumpets, Trombones, and Tubas; Timpani, Organ; and Strings: Violins, Violas, Cellos, and Contrabasses, for the oratorio.

For this selection, Mendelssohn utilizes Woodwind instruments and Strings.

"Is Not His Word Like a Fire?"

from *Elijah* by F. Mendelssohn

After the previous piece, No. 14, and the manifestations of divine fire, the people realize whose god is the true God and proclaim, "The Lord, he is God" ("Der HERR ist Gott") in 1 Kings 18:39. The aria "Ist nicht des Herrn Wort wie ein Feuer?" in German is sung by Elijah in Scene 3 of Part I, No. 17, after ordering the execution of the Priests of Baal, No. 16 (1 Kings 18:40).

As previously mentioned, because of the common theme of "fire," it is highly probable that in composing this aria, Mendelssohn took as his model Handel's "Refiner's fire" from the aria "But Who May Abide the Day of His Coming?" from *Messiah*.

Text

The lyrics are based on Jeremiah 23:29 and Psalms 7:11-12.

Schubring's Libretto	The Bible (KJV)
The Aria	
Is not His word like a fire; and like a hammer that breaketh the rock into pieces?	[29]Is not my word like as a fire? saith the LORD; and like a hammer that breaketh the rock in pieces? (KJV: Jeremiah 23:29)
For God is angry with the wicked every day; and if the wicked turn not, the Lord will whet His sword; and He hath bent His bow, and made it ready.	[11]God judgeth the righteous, and God is angry with the wicked every day. [12]If he turn not, he will whet his sword; he hath bent his bow, and made it ready. (KJV: Psalm 7:11 - 12)

Table 7. Text of "Is Not His Word Like a Fire?"

Performance Notes

The aria "Is not His Word Like a Fire" is a typical operatic rage aria marked *Allegro con fuoco e marcato* and in A minor, including wide skips, demanding melismas, and agitated orchestral parts—similar to Handel's rage arias.

This aria requires skillful vocal techniques due to the many leaps (both up and down), various dynamic changes, and some energized phrases, including several melismas. For the words "fire," "word," and "breaketh," Mendelssohn utilizes challenging melismas that are relatively briefer rather that Handel's rage ones. The performer should sing the words in melismas with proper vowels; [ɑ] vowel for "fire," [ɜ] vowel for "word," and [ɛ] vowel for the first syllable of "breaketh." Also, the performer should sing all the eighth notes of melismas with an energized and determined tone color in order to portray God's fury.

This aria takes approximately two minutes and thirty seconds to perform. The vocal range is from C3 to F4, but owing to the many leaps and chromatic scales, the *tessitura* itself is not easily determined. The form is through-composed, with no whole section repeated despite repeated words and phrases throughout.

Mendelssohn always places the words "fire" and "rock" on strong beats, but the first word "is" of the phrase, "Is not His word like a fire," he puts on weak beats. This suggests that Mendelssohn knew English well in terms of where the musical and textual accents fall, just as Handel did (Ex. 14). Ironically, they were both German-born composers.

At the beginning of the aria, the first four measures of orchestral accompaniment are almost identical to the following four measures as Mendelssohn sets the first phrase of the text, "Is not His word like a fire?" (mm. 3-5), from Jeremiah 23:29, and "And like a hammer that breaketh the rock" (mm. 7-9) in order to emphasize as well as manifest God's fury (Ex. 14).

Example 14. *Elijah*, "Is Not His Word Like a Fire?" mm. 1-9.

The aria finishes with the question "Is not His word like a hammer that breaketh the rock?" from 82 to 86, and especially from mm. 82 to 84, with voice only without any accompaniment. The tempo marking is *più lento*, thus providing a dramatic ending akin to a cadenza in an operatic aria (Ex. 15). Since the first note of this section is F4, the performer should encounter a vowel modification of the word "is."

Example 15. *Elijah*, "Is Not His Word Like a Fire?" mm. 82-86.

Orchestration

Mendelssohn uses Clarinets, Horns, and Strings for this selection.

"It Is Enough"

from *Elijah* by F. Mendelssohn

Since Elijah orders the execution of all the priests (including Jezebel's), Jezebel retaliates by issuing an order to kill Elijah (1 Kings 19:2). Elijah immediately runs away from Jezebel's immediate reach to Beersheba[78] in Judah (1 Kings 19:3). Eventually, Elijah begins this aria, "It Is Enough," praying for his death, as he says, "It is enough; now, O LORD, take away my life; for I am not better than my fathers" (1 Kings 19:4).

Text

The lyrics are from 1 Kings 19:4, 10 and Job 7:16 with the A section based on two verses, namely 1 Kings 19:4 and Job 7:16; and the B section based on 1 Kings 19:10.

Schubring's Libretto	**The Bible (KJV)**
The Aria	
It is enough; O Lord, now take away my life, for I am not better than my fathers!	[4]But he himself went a day's journey into the wilderness, and came and sat down under a juniper tree: and he requested for himself that he might die; and said, It is enough; now, O LORD, take away my life; for I am not better than my fathers. (1 Kings 19:4)
I desire to live no longer; now let me die, for my days are but vanity!	[16]I loathe it; I would not live alway: let me alone; for my days are vanity. (Job 7:16)
I have been very jealous for the Lord God of Hosts! For the children of Israel have broken Thy covenant, and thrown down Thine altars, and slain all Thy prophets — slain them with the sword; and I, even I, only am left; and they seek my life to take it away.	[10]And he said, I have been very jealous for the LORD God of hosts: for the children of Israel have forsaken thy covenant, thrown down thine altars, and slain thy prophets with the sword; and I, even I only, am left; and they seek my life, to take it away. (1 Kings 19:10)

Table 8. Text of "It Is Enough"

80

Performance Notes

The dramatic events of Scene 2 (Nos. 25–32) penetrate deeply into Elijah's despondent soul as he hides in the wilderness from Jezebel's soldiers. The aria "It Is Enough" appears in Scene 2 of Part II, No. 26, sung by Elijah (baritone). The aria can be classified as a prayer-like aria that exhibits Elijah's fear of death and suffering in the wilderness. Even though Elijah has already experienced God's fiery power and knows who He is, he is still fearful of Jezebel's threat to have him killed.

The song is in ternary form (ABA), with tempos marked *Adagio* (A), *Molto allegro vivace* (B), and *Adagio* (A). The aria takes approximately six minutes to perform and remains in the key of F♯ minor throughout, but meters are 3/4 (A), 4/4 (B), and 3/4 (A).

Prior to the song, Elijah declares his escape into the wilderness in his recitative, No. 25, "Though stricken, they have not grieved! Tarry here, my servant; the Lord be with thee. I journey hence to the wilderness." After this six-measure recitative, there are four measures of postlude that contain recitatives by Obadiah and Elijah, signifying the time lapsed for Elijah's escape. There are nine measures of orchestral introduction before the aria starts in measure ten, where Elijah's weariness and feelings of hopelessness are indicated by a slow tempo (*Adagio*), and walking-pace orchestral accompaniments to a mournful cello solo. Thus, the performer should echo the mood of the introduction with less volume (*piano*) for the A section. The performer should also demonstrate in each section a differentiation of tone colors, the two A sections reflecting sorrow and hopelessness, characterized by a more breathy sound that represents his fatigue, and the intense and agitated B section reflecting rage and desperation. At the beginning of the B section, Mendelssohn provides two measures of interlude (mm. 46-47) to establish a totally different mood by adding more wind instruments and a faster tempo. However, Mendelssohn does not change the mood suddenly but builds it up gradually from m. 34 with repeating 8th notes and 32nd notes in mm. 43-45. Therefore, the performer should echo this changed mood with louder volume (*forte*) and with more energy.

Orchestration

Mendelssohn makes use of only Strings for the A section; adds Clarinets, Bassoons, Horns, Trombones for the B section; and excludes the Brass (Horns and Trombones) for the last A section (Clarinets, Bassoons, and Strings only).

Conclusion and a Note from the Author

I hope this has been for you a much-needed resource regarding the performance of selected arias for baritone/bass-baritone by George Frideric Handel and Felix Mendelssohn. Notwithstanding the formal structure of the music of both periods and composers represented, the arias can still be performed with a wide range of emotion. The triangulation of data approach consisting of 1) What the text of the aria is saying; 2) What the character singing the aria is experiencing in context; and 3) What the composer intends for the given aria as evidenced by the music, is a viable basic template or construct for approaching how these arias might be performed. If you are a voice teacher, this may serve as a useful tool for discovering whether your own personal interpretation can be reasonably supported.

The historical and general biographical background of both Handel and Mendelssohn provides additional corroborating data as to where the emotional content of the arias comes from. As shown earlier, Handel was no stranger to extreme emotion or to the struggles involved in managing often tumultuous relationships with others. Moreover, Mendelssohn was no stranger to persecution, a major theme in both *Paulus* and *Elijah*. As a performer, you may identify with the composer as well as with his music. In other words, the performance in such cases embodies not only the score of the music but also the life experience of the person who created it. Furthermore, the emergence of the oratorio in London, for example, was primarily thrust upon Handel by the changing tastes of London's audience, just as Mendelssohn's conversion to Christianity was thrust upon him by the anti-Semitic sentiments of nineteenth-century Germany. While these observations are not a major finding of the study, they do perhaps explain some additional origins of anger in the arias as the musical expression.

If you are a student with performance questions and lack immediate access to a teacher, I have provided principles of voice pedagogy needed to perform the notes themselves by identifying areas of challenge for the singer. Moreover, the establishing of the "singer's body" adds a physical reminder that complements mental and spiritual preparation.

I'd like to share a story from my life. Just as many of you find it useful to connect with composers' life experiences, so too I access my own experiences when preparing mentally, emotionally, and spiritually for a voice performance. The following is one of those experiences:

I do not remember the exact date and time, but the day was very beautiful and the sun was shining brightly. My wife and I went to our regular checkup of our first baby, Joseph, to see if our baby was doing well and growing up properly. The ob-gyn applied some liquid gel to my wife's belly in order to examine her with an ultrasound device. She explained the locations of his head, arms, legs, etc. As my wife and I had a fun and enjoyable time, suddenly, our doctor's face became serious. Without saying a word, she examined my baby's heart numerous times. Over a long period of time, she started to report what she had found on my baby's heart. She informed us that it is very rare, but she had seen it before. What she found was a tiny dot in Joseph's heart, and that it was not good at all. She suggested that we need to go to a larger hospital in Indianapolis to see a specialist who would inspect Joseph more thoroughly with a higher quality ultrasound device. The special doctor would tell us more precisely about it. She also mentioned that this abnormality would, in fact, cause a serious heart disease to our baby. Our happy time suddenly became a dark and hopeless time. On the way to our home, my wife cried very hard and I do not remember how I drove at all. In addition to that, we had to wait at least one more month to make an appointment with the specialist in Indianapolis. What as only one month felt like longer than a year!

The only thing we could do was pray. I still remember that I told my Lord that if the sickness could transfer to me from my baby so that my baby would never suffer at all, I would do it. My wife and I prayed whenever we could and every time we did, we prayed with a fervent desire to get rid of the disease from my son's heart. We never forgot each prayer time that the Lord comforted us while we were praying together. A month later, we went to the hospital and wanted to know what was going on with my baby's heart. The specialist doctor welcomed us with a big smile and directed us to the ultrasound exam room. She began to examine and apply some liquid gel to my wife's belly before the ultrasound. While she was examining our baby's heart, she said nothing. She looked very serious and cautious because she already knew why we were there. I just sat beside my wife's bed and kept praying as I looked at the screen of the ultrasound. A few minutes passed, and the doctor opened her mouth and reported to us that she did not discover anything wrong or any spot at all! She said, "it looks like a normal and healthy baby." We were speechless, but we knew Who healed my son. He, the Lord of Lords and King of Kings, did it! He heard our prayer. He surely did. I still remember this moment whenever I share this story with people. I always tear up, but I have a grateful heart. Thus, God gave us a serious time to come together and used the time for us to mature and come near to the Lord. Sometimes we simply forget that the Lord will always be with us no matter how we feel and what we do.

Furthermore, with my second child, Elizabeth, we also faced a similar situation. We were at her 6-year-old checkup when the pediatrician said that Elizabeth had a genetic illness, and that we should again see a special doctor. It was confirmed that she had a genetic disorder that doctors did not have a cure for. At this moment, I felt like the world was ending once again. However, we prayed very hard and asked the Lord that Elizabeth would live a long and happy life. My family and I are still praying every day for her, and thankfully, Elizabeth does not experience any hardships or severe effects of her illness. There are many possible symptoms that she could experience due to the genetic disorder, including scoliosis, optic gliomas, and cognitive differences. In our most recent doctor's visit, the doctor said she is in excellent shape, and especially that her eyes are healthier than an average child. Elizabeth is one of the honor students in her school as well. She has not fully healed yet, and still possesses the possibility of experiencing the symptoms and sufferings of her illness. I believe that God will keep His eyes upon her physically as well as spiritually. We always pray for her, and she is very healthy now, as a result of prayer.

The Lord hears our prayers when we pray with all our heart and we should always trust in Him. His Word tells us:

"Call upon Me in the day of trouble; I will deliver you, and you shall glorify Me." (NKJV: Psalm 50:15)

"Be anxious for nothing, but in everything by prayer and supplication, with thanksgiving, let your requests be made known to God; and the peace of God, which surpasses all understanding, will guard your hearts and minds through Christ Jesus." (NKJV: Philippians 4:6-7)

Everyone has a unique experience with the Lord like mine. When performing a song or an oratorio aria, I will always connect my experiences with the Lord, which I mentioned earlier, to assist in expressing each composer's intended moods and emotions, such as rage, lament, and prayer (reverence). For example, when I sing the aria "It is enough" sung by Elijah; he already knew well who God is and what He can do. However, when Elijah was threatened to be put to death, he just forgot about God and expressed a hopeless and desperate state. Whenever I sing this sort of song, I tend to always recall the moment when we found out our children's health issues and that something seemed beyond hope. Furthermore, it applies to other kinds of emotions, such as lament and rage as well.

Sample Lecture-Recital Program

The author performed the following program on April 8, 2018 in Brookes Chapel at Shorter University in Rome, Georgia. The order of the arias is based on the premiere dates and languages.

Alexander's Feast	George Frideric Handel
Revenge, Timotheus cries	(1685–1759)

Saul

What do I hear? … To Him ten thousands!
With rage I shall burst, his praises to hear!

A Serpent, in my bosom warm'd
Has he escap'd my rage

Messiah

Thus saith the Lord … But who may abide the day of His coming?

Why do the nations so furiously rage?

Joshua

The walls are levell'd … See, the raging flames arise

Intermission

Paulus	Felix Mendelssohn
Vertilge sie, Herr Zebaoth	(1809–1847)

Gott, sei mir gnädig

Elijah

Draw near, all ye people… Lord God of Abraham

Is not his word like a fire?

It is enough

Endnotes

1   Gerald Abraham, *Handel: A Symposium* (London: Oxford University Press, 1954), 262–63.

2   Ibid., 3.

3   Translated from Johann Christoph von Dreyhaupt, *Pagus neletici et nudzici...* (Halle: Verlag des Waysenhauses, 1755), 625.

4   John Mainwaring, *Memoirs of the Life of the Late George Frederic Handel* (London: R. & J. Dodsley, 1760), 2, 15.

5   Victor Schoelcher, *The Life of Handel,* trans. James Lowe (London: Robert Cocks & Co., 1857), 6.

6   William Archie Knowles, "Performer's Analysis of the Bass Roles in Selected Old Testament Narrative English Oratorios of George Frideric Handel" (D.M.A. diss., The Southern Baptist Theological Seminary, 2003), 8.

7   Winton Dean and Anthony Hicks, *The New Grove Handel* (New York: W. W. Norton, 1983), 2.

8   George Predota, "Saved by 'Cleopatra' Handel-Mattheson Duel," *Interlude*, (July 02, 2014), accessed July 4, 2017, http://www.interlude.hk/front/saved-by-cleopatrahandel-mattheson-duel/.

9   Mainwaring, *Memoirs of the Life of the Late George Frederic Handel*, 35.

10   Julian Herbage, "The Oratorios," in *Handel: A Symposium*, ed. Gerald Abraham (London: Oxford University Press, 1969), 68.

11   Donald Burrows, *The Cambridge Companion to Handel* (New York: Cambridge University Press, 1997), introduction, Kindle.

12   Ruth Smith, *Handel's Oratorios and Eighteenth-Century Thought* (New York: Cambridge University Press, 1995), 18.

13   Richard Luckett, *Handel's Messiah: A Celebration* (New York: Harcourt Brace & Company, 1992), 18.

14   Donald Burrows, *Handel*, Master Musicians Series, 2nd ed. (Oxford: Oxford University Press, 2012), 92.

15   David Poultney, *Studying Music History: Learning, Reasoning, and Writing about Music History and Literature*, 2nd ed. (Upper Saddle River, NJ: Pearson, 1995), 103.

16   R. Larry Todd, *Mendelssohn: A Life in Music* (Oxford: Oxford University Press, 2003), 33.

17   Ibid., 35–36.

18   Leon Plantinga, *Romantic Music: A History of Musical Style in Nineteenth-Century Europe*, Norton Introduction to Music History (New York : W. W. Norton, 1984), 19.

19   Ibid., 247.

20   "Fanny Mendelssohn Hensel, 1805-1847," web page, *Library of Congress, Washington, D.C. 20540 USA*, accessed July 10, 2017, https://www.loc.gov/item/ihas.200156440/.

21   R. Larry Todd, "Discovering Music - 2 Minutes with R. Larry Todd," accessed July 10, 2017, http://www.oxfordpresents.com/ms/todd/category/vid/.

22   Nancy B. Reich, "The Power of Class: Fanny Hensel," In *Mendelssohn and His World*, ed. R. Larry Todd (Princeton, NJ: Princeton University Press, 1991), 92.

23   Ibid., 87.

24   Plantinga, *Romantic Music: A History of Musical Style in Nineteenth-Century Europe*, 250.

25   Todd, *Mendelssohn*, 73.

26   Plantinga, *Romantic Music: A History of Musical Style in Nineteenth-Century Europe*, 12.

27   Ibid., 253.

28   Hellmuth Christian Wolff, "Mendelssohn and Handel," trans. Ernest Sanders and Luise Eitel, *The Musical Quarterly* 45, no. 2, (1959): 175.

29   Ibid., 178–79.

30   Plantinga, *Romantic Music: A History of Musical Style in Nineteenth-Century Europe*, 251.

31   Todd, *Mendelssohn*, 337.

32   Donald Jay Grout and Hermine Weigel Williams, *A Short History of Opera*, 4ᵗʰ ed. (New York: Columbia University Press, 2003), 426.

33   Colin Eatock, "Lyric Misgivings," *Opera* (February 2009), accessed July 1, 2017, http://www.colineatock.com/mendelssohn-opera.html.

34   R. Larry Todd, "Mendelssohn, Felix," *Grove Music Online*, accessed July 4, 2017.

35   It is often shortened to "ad-lib," meaning of "as you desire." In music, it means to improvise a melodic line.

36   ***Affektenlehre*** (Doctrine of Affections) —A theory that arose during the Baroque period: A belief that different musical moods could and should be used to influence the emotions of the listeners. The principal aim of music is to stir up the passions or affections. Only one affection was attempted to be expressed per piece or movement. For instance, happiness would be awakened through the use of faster notes and major sonorities, sadness through minor keys and slower movement, anger through loudness and harsh, discordant harmonies.

37   John Walter Hill, *Baroque Music: Music in Western Europe, 1580-1750* (New York : W. W. Norton, 2005), 396.

38   Ibid.

39   Roger Warren Ardrey, "The Influence of the Extended Latin Sacred Works of Giacomo Carissimi on the Biblical Oratorios of George Frederic Handel" (Ph.D. diss., Catholic University of America, 1963), 36.

40   Ibid., 25.

41   Ibid., 110.

42   Tim Carter, *Monteverdi's Musical Theatre* (New Haven: Yale University Press, 2002), 250.

43   Ardrey, "The Influence of the Extended Latin Sacred Works of Giacomo Carissimi on the Biblical Oratorios of George Frederic Handel," 89–90.

44   Poultney, *Studying Music History*, 76.

45   Hill, *Baroque Music: Music in Western Europe, 1580-1750*, 469.

46   Smith, *Handel's Oratorios and Eighteenth-Century Thought*, 93–94.

47   Howard E. Smither, "Oratorio," *Grove Music Online*, accessed August 13, 2017, http://www.oxfordmusiconline.com/subscriber/article/grove/music/20397.

48   Howard E. Smither, *A History of the Oratorio, Vol. 2: The Oratorio in the Baroque Era, Protestant Germany and England* (Chapel Hill: University of North Carolina Press, 1977), 178.

49   Smith, *Handel's Oratorios and Eighteenth-Century Thought*, 20.

50   Meaning "a crowd" or "a group of people"

51   Poultney, *Studying Music History*, 79–80.

52   Smith, *Handel's Oratorios and Eighteenth-Century Thought*, 87.

53   Howard E. Smither, *A History of the Oratorio, Vol. 4: The Oratorio in the Nineteenth and Twentieth Centuries* (Chapel Hill: University of North Carolina Press, 2000), 48.

54   F. G. Edwards, "First Performances. I. Mendelssohn's 'St. Paul,'" *The Musical Times and Singing Class Circular* 32, no. 577 (1891): 137.

55   F. G. Edwards, "First Performances. IV. Mendelssohn's 'Elijah.' (Concluded)," *The Musical Times and Singing Class Circular* 32, no. 584 (1891): 589.

56   Edwards, "First Performances. I. Mendelssohn's 'St. Paul,'" 137

57   Smither, "Oratorio," *Grove Music Online.*

58   Smither, *A History of the Oratorio, Vol. 4: The Oratorio in the Nineteenth and Twentieth Centuries*, 50.

59   Smither, "Oratorio," *Grove Music Online.*

60   Ibid.

61   Smither, *A History of the Oratorio, vol. 2: The Oratorio in the Baroque Era, Protestant Germany and England*, 214.

62   Humphrey F. Sassoon, "J S Bach's Musical Offering and the Source of Its Theme: Royal Peculiar," *The Musical Times* 144, no. 1885 (2003): 38–39.

63   Smither, *A History of the Oratorio, vol. 2: The Oratorio in the Baroque Era, Protestant Germany and England*, 215.

64   Ibid., 2:217.

65   Smither, *A History of the Oratorio, vol. 2: The Oratorio in the Baroque Era, Protestant Germany and England*, 219.

66   Weston H. Noble and Paul Salamunovich, *Creating the Special World: A Collection of Lectures*, ed. Steven M. Demorest (Chicago: G I A Pubns, 2005), 82.

67   Paul Henry Lang, *George Frideric Handel* (New York: W. W. Norton, 1966), 548.

68   Luckett, *Handel's Messiah: A Celebration.* Introduction.

69   Richard Miller, *The Structure of Singing: System and Art in Vocal Technique* (New York: Schirmer Books, 1986), 99.

70   Smither, *A History of the Oratorio, vol. 2: The Oratorio in the Baroque Era, Protestant Germany and England*, 261.

71   Richard Miller, *Securing Baritone, Bass-Baritone, and Bass Voices* (New York: Oxford University Press, 2008), 94.

72   Smither, *A History of the Oratorio, Vol. 4: The Oratorio in the Nineteenth and Twentieth Centuries*, 150.

73   Ibid., 152.

74   Ibid.

75   Ibid., 166.

76   Ibid., 166–167.

77   Baal and Asherah are false gods that are part of the Canaanite religion.

78   The Desert of Beersheba appears several times in the Old Testament (including Genesis 21, 26, and 28) in different contexts. It was not only Elijah's refuge (1 Kings 19:3), but also Hagar and her son's (Genesis 21:14).

Bibliography

Abraham, Gerald, ed. *Handel: A Symposium.* London: Oxford University Press, 1969.

Anderson, Matthew T., and Kevin Hawkes. *Handel, Who Knew What He Liked.* Cambridge, MA: Candlewick Press, 2001.

Ardrey, Roger Warren. "The Influence of the Extended Latin Sacred Works of Giacomo Carissimi on the Biblical Oratorios of George Frideric Handel." Ph.D. diss., Catholic University of America, 1963.

Armstrong, Thomas. *Mendelssohn's 'Elijah.'* London: Oxford University Press, 1931.

Avison, Charles, and John Jortin. *An Essay on Musical Expression.* London: Lockyer Davis, 1775.

Bauer, Karen Tillotson. *The Essentials of Beautiful Singing: A Three-Step Kinesthetic Approach.* Lanham: Scarecrow Press, 2013.

Buelow, George J. "Johann Mattheson and the Invention of the Affektenlehre." In *New Mattheson Studies*, edited by George J. Buelow and Hans Joachim Marx, 393-408. Cambridge: Cambridge University Press, 1983.

Bukofzer, Manfred F. *Music in the Baroque Era: From Monteverdi to Bach.* New York: W. W. Norton, 1947.

Burrows, Donald James. *Handel.* Master Musicians Series. 2nd ed. Oxford: Oxford University Press, 2012.

———. *Handel and the English Chapel Royal.* Oxford: Oxford University Press, 2005.

———. *Handel: Messiah.* New York: Cambridge University Press, 1991.

———, ed. *The Cambridge Companion to Handel.* New York: Cambridge University Press, 1997.

———, Helen Coffey, John Greenacombe, and Anthony Hicks, comps. and eds. *George Frideric Handel: Collected Documents. Vol. 1: 1609-1725.* Cambridge: Cambridge University Press, 2014.

Burton, Anthony, ed. *A Performer's Guide to Music of the Baroque Period.* London: Associated Board of the Royal Schools of Music, 2002.

Carter, Tim. *Monteverdi's Musical Theatre.* New Haven: Yale University Press, 2002.

Celletti, Rodolfo. *A History of Bel Canto.* Translated by Friderick Fuller. Oxford; Clarendon Press, 1991.

Clark, Jonathan Charles Douglas. *English Society, 1660-1832: Religion, Ideology and Politics during the Ancien Regime.* New York: Cambridge University Press, 2000.

Cooper, John Michael. *Felix Mendelssohn Bartholdy: A Research and Information Guide.* 2nd ed. New York: Routledge, 2010.

Dean, Winton. *Handel's Dramatic Oratorios and Masques.* New York: Oxford University Press, 1990.

———. *Handel and the Opera Seria.* Berkeley: University of California Press, 1969.

Dean, Winton, and Anthony Hicks. *The New Grove Handel.* New York: W. W. Norton, 1983.

Dean, Winton, and J. Merrill Knapp. *Handel's Operas, 1704-1726.* Vol. 1. London: Oxford University Press, 1995.

Deutsch, Otto Erich. *Handel: A Documentary Biography.* London: J. M. Dent, 1946.

Donington, Robert. *Baroque Music, Style and Performance: A Handbook.* New York: W. W. Norton, 1982.

Dreyhaupt, Johann Christoph von. *Pagus neletici et nudzici oder ausführliche diplomatisch-historische Beschreibun des… Saal-Creises.* 2. Halle: Verlag des Waysenhauses, 1755.

Eatock, Colin. "Lyric Misgivings." *Opera* (February 2009). Accessed July 1, 2017. http://www.colineatock.com/mendelssohn-opera.html.

Edwards, Friderick George, "First Performances. I. Mendelssohn's 'St. Paul.'" *The Musical Times and Singing Class Circular* 32, no. 577 (1891).

———. "First Performances. IV. Mendelssohn's 'Elijah.' (Concluded)," *The Musical Times and Singing Class Circular* 32, no. 584 (1891).

———. *The History of Mendelssohn's Oratorio Elijah.* New York: AMS Press, 1976.

"Fanny Mendelssohn Hensel, 1805-1847." Web Page. *Library of Congress, Washington, D.C. 20540 USA.* Accessed July 10, 2017. https://www.loc.gov/item/ihas.200156440/.

Grout, Donald J., and Hermine Weigel Williams. *A Short History of Opera.* 4th ed. New York: Columbia University Press, 2003.

Handel, George Frideric. *Joshua: Vocal Score.* Van Nuys, CA: Alfred Music, 1985.

———. *Messiah.* Edited by Watkins Shaw. London: Novello, 2003.

———. *Samson.* London: Novello, 2004.

———. *Saul.* Bury St. Edmunds: Novello, 2004.

Handel, George Frideric, and John Dryden. *Ode for St. Cecilia's Day: (HWV 76): ST or SAT soloists and SATB chorus.* Edited by Donald Burrows. London: Novello, 2009.

Handel, George Frideric, and J. M. Diack. *Saul: An Oratorio.* New York: Fischer, 1930.

Harris, Ellen T. *Handel as Orpheus: Voice and Desire in the Chamber Cantatas.* Cambridge MA: Harvard University Press, 2004.

Herbage, Julian. "The Oratorios." In *Handel: A Symposium,* edited by Gerald Abraham, 66-131. London: Oxford University Press, 1969.

Hicks, Anthony. "Handel, George Frideric," *Grove Music Online.* Accessed August 10, 2017. http://www.oxfordmusiconline.com/grovemusic.

Hill, John Walter. *Baroque Music: Music in Western Europe, 1580-1750.* New York: W. W. Norton, 2005.

Hiller, Ferdinand, M. E. von Glehn, and Joel Sachs. *Mendelssohn: Letters and Recollections.* New York: Vienna House, 1972.

Hogwood, Christopher. *Handel.* Rev. ed. London: Thames & Hudson, 2007.

Keates, Jonathan. *Handel: The Man & His Music.* Rev. ed. London: Bodley Head, 2008.

Knowles, William Archie. "Performer's Analysis of the Bass Roles in Selected Old Testament Narrative English Oratorios of George Frideric Handel." D.M.A. diss., The Southern Baptist Theological Seminary, 2003.

Lang, Paul Henry. *George Frideric Handel.* New York: W. W. Norton, 1966.

Larsen, Jens Peter. *Handel's Messiah: Origins, Composition, Sources.* New York: W. W. Norton, 1972.

LaRue, C. S. *Handel and His Singers: The Creation of the Royal Academy Operas, 1720-1728.* Oxford: Clarendon Press, 1995.

Luckett, Richard. *Handel's* Messiah: *A Celebration*. New York: Harcourt Brace & Company, 1992.

Mainwaring, John. *Memoirs of the Life of the Late George Frideric Handel*. London: R & J Dodesley, 1760.

Mendelssohn-Bartholdy, Felix. *Elias*, Op. 70. Klavierauszug. Stuttgart: Carus-Verlag, 1996.

———. *Saint Paul*, Op. 36. Vocal Score. New York: G. Schirmer, Inc.

Meynell, Hugo Anthony. *The Art of Handel's operas*. Vol. 1. New York: Edwin Mellen Press, 1986.

Miller, Richard. *The Structure of Singing: System and Art in Vocal Technique*. New York: Schirmer Books, 1986.

———. *Securing Baritone, Bass-Baritone, and Bass Voices*. New York: Oxford University Press, 2008.

Moses, Don V., Robert W. Demaree Jr, and Allen F. Ohmes. *Face to Face with Orchestra and Chorus: A Handbook for Choral Conductors*. 2nd, expanded ed. Bloomington: Indiana University Press, 2004.

Moshansky, Mozelle. *Mendelssohn, His Life and Times*. New York: Hippocrene Books, 1982.

Myers, Robert Manson and George Frideric Handel. *Handel's Messiah: A Touchstone of Taste*. New York: Macmillan Co., 1948.

Noble, Weston H., and Paul Salamunovich. *Creating the Special World: A Collection of Lectures*. Edited by Steven M. Demorest. Chicago: G I A Pubns, 2005.

Parker, Mary Ann. *G. F. Handel: A Guide to Research*. New York: Routledge, 2005.

Plantinga, Leon. *Romantic Music: A History of Musical Style in Nineteenth-Century Europe*. New York: W. W. Norton, 1984.

Poultney, David. *Studying Music History: Learning, Reasoning, and Writing about Music History and Literature.* Upper Saddle River, NJ: Pearson, 1996.

Predota, Georg. "Saved by 'Cleopatra' Handel-Matheson Duel." *Interlude* (July 20, 2014). Accessed July 4, 2017. http://www.interlude.hk/front/saved-by-cleopatrahandel-mattheson-duel/#.

Sassoon, Humphrey F., "J S Bach's Musical Offering and the Source of Its Theme: Royal Peculiar," *The Musical Times* 144, no. 1885 (2003): 38-39.

Schoelcher, Victor. *The Life of Handel.* Translated by James Lowe. London: Robert Cocks & Co., 1857.

Seaton, Douglass. *The Mendelssohn Companion.* Westport, CT: Greenwood Press, 2001.

Shrock, Dennis. *Handel's Messiah: A Performance Practice Handbook.* Chicago: GIA Publications, 2013.

Smith, Ruth. *Handel's Oratorios and Eighteenth-Century Thought.* Cambridge; New York: Cambridge University Press, 1995.

Smither, Howard E. *A History of the Oratorio, Vol. 2: The Oratorio in the Baroque Era.* Chapel Hill: University of North Carolina Press, 1977.

———. *A History of the Oratorio, Vol. 4: The Oratorio in the Nineteenth and Twentieth Centuries.* Chapel Hill: University of North Carolina Press, 2000.

———. "Oratorio." *Grove Music Online.* Accessed August 13, 2017. http://www.oxfordmusiconline.com/subscriber/article/grove/music/20397.

Sposato, Jeffrey S. "Mendelssohn, 'Paulus,' and the Jews: A Response to Leon Botstein and Michael Steinberg." *The Musical Quartely* 83, no 2. (1999): 280-91.

Temperley, Nicholas. "Mendelssohn's Influence on English Music." *Music & Letters,* no. 3, (1962): 224-33.

Todd, R. Larry. "Discovering Music - 2 Minutes with R. Larry Todd." Accessed July 10, 2017. http://www.oxfordpresents.com/ms/todd/category/vid/.

————. *Mendelssohn: A Life in Music*. New York: Oxford University Press, 2003.

————. *Mendelssohn and His World*. Princeton, NJ: Princeton University Press, 1991.

————. *Mendelssohn's Musical Education: A Study and Edition of His Exercises in Composition*. Cambridge: Cambridge University Press, 2009.

————. "Mendelssohn (-Bartholdy), (Jacob Ludwig) Felix." *Grove Music Online*. Accessed July 4, 2017. http://www.oxfordmusiconline.com/grovemusic.

Van Camp, Leonard. *A Practical Guide for Performing, Teaching & Singing "Messiah."* Edited by Scott Foss. Dayton, OH: Lorenz Corporation, 1993.

Various. *Sacred Songs and Arias for Baritone/Bass (The Ultimate Collection) CD Sheet Music*. Milwaukee, WI: Hal Leonard, 2008.

Walters, Richard. *The Oratorio Anthology*. Milwaukee, WI: H. Leonard, 1994.

Werner, Jack. *Mendelssohn's "Elijah": A Historical and Analytical Guide to the Oratorio*. London: MSM, 1965.

Wolff, Hellmuth Christian. "Mendelssohn and Handel." Translated by Ernest Sanders and Luise Eitel. *The Musical Quarterly* 45, no. 2 (1959): 175-90.

About the Author

A native of South Korea, Yuman Lee serves as an Assistant Professor of Music at Shorter University in Rome, Georgia. He teaches lyric diction, voice pedagogy, opera literature, voice seminar, and private voice.

Dr. Lee holds a Doctor of Musical Arts in Vocal Performance from the School of Church Music, Southwestern Baptist Theological Seminary, Fort Worth, TX. As a recipient of James Mckinney Outstanding Performer Award from the President of SWBTS, he performed with the Fort Worth Symphony Orchestra. While there, he was selected as a vocal arts honors recitalist 2009-2010, 2010-2011, and 2013-2014.

Prior to moving to Texas, Lee received his Master of Music degree from the Thornton School of Music, University of Southern California where he performed numerous operas, including Le Nozze di Figaro, Don Giovanni, I Capuleti e i Montecchi, and various opera scenes. Lee performed the role of Don Pasquale in Donizetti's Don Pasquale in Italy during the summer program in Viterbo and Rome. He was inducted to Pi Kappa Lambda, the honor society of music, in 2010 and is also a member of the National Association of Teachers of Singing. His students consistently place at the top of their divisions in state and regional NATS auditions.

Prior to moving to Los Angeles, Lee received his Bachelor of Music degree in Vocal Arts, with a minor in piano, from Kyung Hee University, Seoul, South Korea. As a junior, Lee directed a hundred-voice ensemble. As a senior, aside from the regular courses within the music school, Lee worked on La Boheme, Don Giovanni, and La Traviata in numerous opera workshops. In addition, at a graduation ceremony, he won the Distinguished Service Award from the President of the university.

Prior to moving to Georgia, Lee served as a Minister of Music at Ridglea Baptist Church, Fort Worth, TX. Yuman Lee is an active soloist, having performed in the United States, Europe, as well as South Korea.

"My teaching philosophy has guided the conclusion that each student is a unique person, having incompatible strengths, weakness, and intentions to the voice studio. I believe that the most critical ability students must learn is the skill to acquire a knowledge of the art of singing and create independently so that after they leave the school setting, they can engage in music and intellectual activities on their own. My purpose is to help my students be their own best teacher and to support student's growth into human beings who will contribute their knowledge and talents to society. I hope for students to comprehend the mind-body connection involved in singing as well as I want them to experience singing as a great pleasure and natural expression of their feeling."

Dr. Lee is married to Myung Hee Ha, and he has three children; Joseph, Elizabeth, and Anna.

- **Opera** – Don Giovanni, Cosi Fan Tutte, Le Nozze di Figaro, Don Pasquale, The Rape of Lucrecia, I Capuleti e I Montecchi, La Boheme, and more.
- **Oratorio and Sacred work** – Bach BWV 80 (Ein feste Burg ist Gott), BWV 82 (Ich habe genug), Messiah, Missa in tempore belli, Creation, Requiem (Mozart and Verdi), Elijah, Ein Deutsches Requiem, Fantasia on Christmas Carols, Christmas Oratorio, and more.

Praise for Yuman Lee and *It Is Enough!*

Dr. Lee has established himself as a master musician enhanced by faith. His general approach to the use of emotion—taken from life experience— in performance can prove valuable to all musicians. He moves from the general to the specific as he provides principles of voice pedagogy to assist in performance of his selected arias.

Dr. John D. Reams
Dean
Shorter University
School of Fine & Performing Arts

I have had the privilege of serving with Dr. Yuman Lee in ministry. His singing, worship leadership, and conducting lift the congregation into the presence of The Holy One. Exceptional musical skills and knowledge are kissed by the presence of God. I attribute his uniquely blessed abilities to two prominent qualities in this man, sensitivity and reverence. Dr. Lee is profoundly in touch with the moods and feelings of individuals and the congregation as a whole. He also believes and feels what he is singing and this is tangible in his musical expressions. His reverence for God expressed in his words and manner is contagious. His prayers are as impactful as his music. Dr. Lee has left an indelible impression on our congregation! It has been a great privilege to serve with him in ministry. It is an even greater privilege to call him my friend.

Scott T. Cox
Senior Pastor
Ridglea Baptist Church
Fort Worth, TX

This publication is a great resource for voice teachers and singers alike and will prove to be advantageous for musical, mental, emotional and spiritual preparation which will enhance the performance of these arias for baritone and bass-baritone by Handel and Mendelssohn.

Dr. Angela Cofer
Professor of Voice
Southwestern Baptist Theological Seminary
School of Church Music

Dr. Lee has given teachers and students a valuable musical and vocal resource in this book. Most significantly, though, he has gone beyond the expected musical approaches to emphasize the emotional and spiritual depth of the music. This book will hopefully deepen your appreciation of this great music and enable you to teach and perform it with new fervor.

Dr. Alan Wingard
Dean Emeritus
Shorter University
School of Fine & Performing Arts

www.ingramcontent.com/pod-product-compliance
Lightning Source LLC
Chambersburg PA
CBHW060418090426
42734CB00011B/2361